Religious Education
The Teacher's Guide

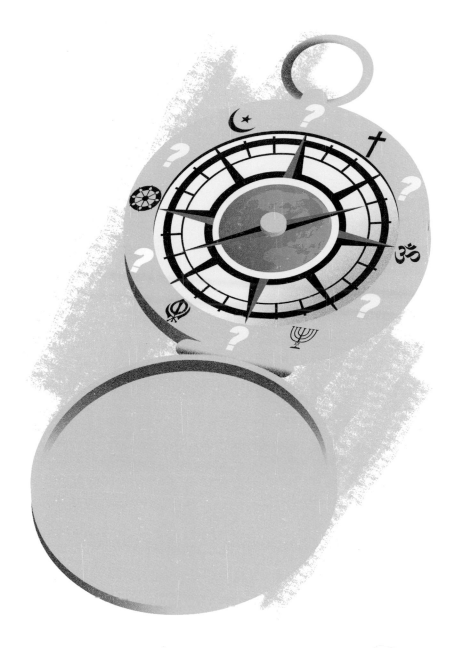

Editor
Stephen Pett

RE Today
Services

RE Today Services, a part of Christian Education, is an ecumenical educational charity which works throughout the United Kingdom.

Its aims are:

• to support religious education in schools

• to increase awareness of the spiritual, moral, social and cultural dimensions of the curriculum

• to articulate Christian perspectives on education.

RE Today Services is committed to the teaching of the major world faiths in religious education, and to an accurate and fair representation of their beliefs, values and practices in all its teaching materials.

RE Today Services fulfils these aims:

• by publishing teaching materials like this resource and background papers, together with a termly magazine *REtoday*, and distributing the *British Journal of Religious Education*

• by offering professional development and consultancy services through its professional staff

• by arranging national and regional courses for teachers, pupils and others interested in education

• by research and curriculum development work

• by sponsoring the work of the National Association of Teachers of RE (NATRE).

Visit our website: www.retoday.org.uk

Written by the RE Today Advisory team: Lat Blaylock, Kate Christopher, Fiona Moss and Stephen Pett.

Edited by Stephen Pett

Illustrations by Neil Webb: neilwebb.net

Designed and typeset by Christian Education Publications

Acknowledgements The Apostles' Creed as taken from *Common Worship: Services and Prayers for the Church of England* is copyright The English Language Liturgical Consultation © ELLC 1988. Used with permission.

Thanks to Susan Leslie, University of Dundee, for her contribution on pp.24–25.

Every effort has been made to gain permission for the inclusion of copyright material. The publishers would be pleased to include correct attribution of any inadvertently unattributed material in subsequent editions, on being contacted by the lawful copyright holder(s).

RE Today are not responsible for the accuracy, content or availability of third-party websites referred to in this publication.

Published by Christian Education Publications, 1020 Bristol Road, Selly Oak, Birmingham B29 6LB

© RE Today Services 2015

ISBN: 978-1-910261-00-2

A CIP catalogue record for this book is available from the British Library.

Printed and bound in the UK by Thames Print, 19 East Portway, Andover, Hants SP10 3LU

Contents

Introduction

Congratulations! By picking up this book you must already have some interest and involvement in Religious Education in schools – and what a great subject it is! It has its challenges, of course, and we will address them in the following pages, but it has so many rich opportunities too.

RE opens up and explores profound questions about meaning, truth, values and identity raised by being alive. It considers diverse responses to these questions, insights from the world's great religious traditions, from non-religious schools of thought, and from pupils themselves. RE is concerned with what matters most in people's lives, and so it visits those moments of great significance (such as birth, commitment, death). It considers questions of right and wrong, how people decide how to live, and the consequences of this on everyday lives. RE explores questions about God, life after death, revelation and the purposes of life. It introduces pupils to reflecting on the world of the spiritual, to consider whether there are matters of value beyond the material world, and how they might contribute to understanding what it means to be human. RE embraces some of the diversity of creative expression of human belief and practice, through arts as well as action. It involves encounter with real people of faith and belief. And it examines belief through a range of connected disciplines, such as philosophy and ethics.

This exciting journey can begin with quality RE in the early years of school, as children wonder at the marvel of life and how people live, asking thoughtful questions and expressing their ideas. At the end of a pupil's school career, this journey will have ranged over the core concepts in a number of religions, how they have an impact on the lives of individuals and communities, taking into account historical and cultural influences as well as political and social realities. Good RE will face up to the challenges and contradictions of religion and belief in today's world, including the 'dark side' of religion: every belief system seems to have potential for both good and bad.

Teaching RE is itself a challenging process. It needs to take account of the personal worldviews of teachers and pupils in open and honest ways. It should present accurately something of the staggering diversity of religion and belief and how it affects people's lives today. It has to consider carefully the needs of pupils – what do they need to know and be able to do as a result of their study? And it needs to be able to engage pupils in ways that enable them to make progress in knowledge, understanding and skills, and support them on their own search for what is true and what is good.

No easy task ... which is why we've written this book – to give you some of the key information and some practical ideas for planning effective, inspiring and challenging RE for pupils from 4 to 19. It ranges from what the law says about RE, through strategies for leading a team of teachers and ideas for creative activities, to some core knowledge in religion and belief. We have written it to enable any teacher of RE, or any subject leader, to address the key issues which face the subject in any school in increasingly thoughtful and effective ways. We hope it will help you face some of the challenges but also seize the opportunities offered by high-quality Religious Education.

Stephen Pett
Editor

Effective subject leadership in RE:
what do you need to know?

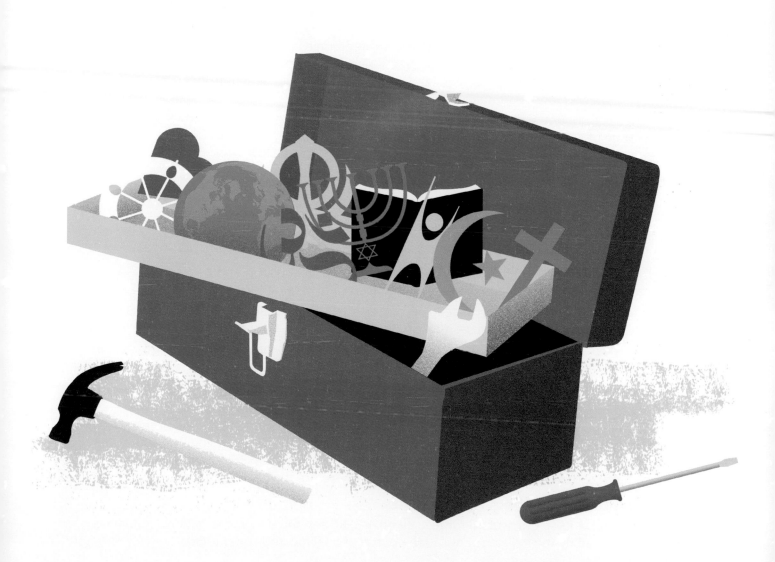

It is important to spend some time in your school or department thinking about what RE is for. Research[1] has shown that where teachers are clear about the purpose of RE, they can be clear about what, how and why they teach, which helps with being clear about pupils' learning, progress and achievement. If teachers are not sure about why they teach RE, it can lead to confusion in planning, teaching and learning, and assessment.

What is the purpose of RE?

There is no single agreed purpose for RE, but you might consider where you think the priorities of the subject lie. Consider these purposes – RE is to enable children and young people to:

- understand religions and beliefs in the world in which we live
- understand people from different backgrounds
- read, understand and interpret religious sources, such as texts or art
- develop understanding about their own identity, beliefs and ways of living
- develop their own considered ideas
- participate in a diverse society
- engage in productive dialogue and debate with people of diverse views and outlooks.

These multiple purposes of RE are not separate or discrete but describe the skills and attributes needed to equip young people for life in a diverse community and a global society. There is great value in spending time as a school or department deciding the purpose of RE. This will stem from your knowledge of the skills and understanding your pupils would benefit from developing as well as your view of local, national and global issues.

If you are clear about the purpose of RE, you can look at what and how you teach. Pages 79–80 offer a range of approaches to RE.

What are the aims of RE?

Once the purpose of RE is established, some more specific aims emerge. In most classes, lessons will have several aims in mind. These aims include helping children and young people to:

- know about different religious traditions and non-religious worldviews
- understand the main beliefs and practices of these traditions
- understand how religious identity influences people's lives
- express views about the nature, value and significance of religion for people and the planet
- consider challenging questions of meaning, purpose, truth, values and commitments, and the answers offered by religions and non-religious worldviews
- develop skills of enquiry, analysis and evaluation and articulate their own considered ideas in relation to these challenging questions.

Which of these aims do you embody most often in your lessons? Are there aims here that you rarely try to meet? If you know your purpose and aims, you can ensure that all of your RE is developed in order to support these. This helps to ensure that you use the limited time available for RE to best effect. Being clear about the knowledge, skills and understandings you want your pupils to gain will always help steer you when planning and assessing RE. Focusing on these aims will also help to increase the challenge to pupils and therefore their achievement.

National guidance on the purpose of RE

As there is no National Curriculum for RE (see pp.4–5, RE and the law), some national guidance has been offered by the Religious Education Council of England and Wales (REC).

---

[1] *Reports Transforming Religious Education* (Ofsted 2010) and *Religious Education: Realising the Potential* (Ofsted 2013).

Below is how the council articulates the purpose and aims of RE. What kind of RE teaching would need to happen in your class to meet these aims and purposes?

Religious education contributes dynamically to children and young people's education in schools by provoking challenging questions about meaning and purpose in life, beliefs about God, ultimate reality, issues of right and wrong and what it means to be human. In RE they learn about and from religions and worldviews[2] in local, national and global contexts, to discover, explore and consider different answers to these questions. They learn to weigh up the value of wisdom from different sources, to develop and express their insights in response, and to agree or disagree respectfully.

Teaching therefore should equip pupils with systematic knowledge and understanding of a range of religions and worldviews, enabling them to develop their ideas, values and identities. It should develop in pupils an aptitude for dialogue so that they can participate positively in our society with its diverse religions and worldviews. Pupils should gain and deploy the skills needed to understand, interpret and evaluate texts, sources of wisdom and authority and other evidence.

They learn to articulate clearly and coherently their personal beliefs, ideas, values and experiences while respecting the right of others to differ.[3]

National guidance on the aims of RE[4]

The curriculum for RE aims to ensure that all pupils:

A Know about and understand a range of religions and worldviews, so that they can:
  - describe, explain and analyse beliefs and practices, recognising the diversity which exists within and between communities and amongst individuals
  - identify, investigate and respond to questions posed, and responses offered by some of the sources of wisdom found in religions and worldviews
  - appreciate and appraise the nature, significance and impact of different ways of life and ways of expressing meaning.

B Express ideas and insights about the nature, significance and impact of religions and worldviews so that they can:
  - explain reasonably their ideas about how beliefs, practices and forms of expression influence individuals and communities
  - express with increasing discernment their personal reflections and critical responses to questions and teachings about identity, diversity, meaning and value, including ethical issues
  - appreciate and appraise varied dimensions of religion or a worldview.

C Gain and deploy the skills needed to engage seriously with religions and worldviews, so that they can:
  - find out about and investigate key concepts and questions of belonging, meaning, purpose and truth, responding creatively
  - enquire into what enables different individuals and communities to live together respectfully for the wellbeing of all
  - articulate beliefs, values and commitments clearly in order to explain why they may be important in their own and other people's lives.

---

[2] The phrase 'religions and worldviews' in the REC's *A Curriculum Framework for Religious Education in England* (REC 2013) and *A Review of Religious Education in England* (REC 2013) refers to Christianity, other principal religions represented in Britain, smaller religious communities and non-religious worldviews such as Humanism. The phrase is meant to be inclusive, and its precise meaning depends on the context in which it occurs, e.g. in terms of belief, practice or identity. Religions might be termed 'religious worldviews', of course.

[3] *A Review of Religious Education in England* (REC 2013), p.14.

[4] Ibid., pp.14–15.

What does the legislation in England say?

RE is for all pupils

- RE must be provided for all registered pupils in state-funded schools in England, including those in the sixth form, unless withdrawn by their parents.[5] It is a necessary part of a 'broad and balanced curriculum'.

- This requirement does not apply for children below compulsory school age (although there are many examples of good practice of RE in nursery classes).

- Special schools should ensure that every pupil receives RE 'as far as is practicable'.[6]

RE is locally determined, not nationally

- A locally agreed syllabus is a statutory syllabus of RE prepared by a local Standing Advisory Council on Religious Education (SACRE) and adopted by a local authority.[7]

- Maintained schools without a religious character should follow the locally agreed syllabus.

- Voluntary aided schools with a religious character should provide RE in accordance with the trust deed or religious designation of the school, unless parents request the locally agreed syllabus.

- Foundation schools and voluntary controlled schools with a religious character should follow the locally agreed syllabus, unless parents request RE in accordance with the trust deed or religious designation of the school.

- RE is also compulsory in faith and non-faith academies and free schools, as set out in their funding agreements. Academies may use their locally agreed syllabus, or a different locally agreed syllabus (with permission of the SACRE concerned), or devise their own curriculum.

RE is multi-faith

- The RE curriculum drawn up by a SACRE, or by an academy or free school, 'shall reflect the fact that the religious traditions in Great Britain are in the main Christian, while taking account of the teaching and practices of the other principal religions represented in Great Britain'.[8]

What does this mean?

As education policy changes, the legal requirement for RE for all registered pupils remains unchanged. RE is an entitlement for all pupils, unless they have been withdrawn by their parents from some or all of the RE curriculum.

 You need to be clear about what RE curriculum is required in your particular type of school. Check that governors, headteachers and teachers know the legal requirement.

 Agreed syllabuses vary in presentation, style and content. Many of them reflect the impact of the 2004 Non-statutory National Framework for RE, produced by the then Qualifications and Curriculum Authority (QCA). Many post-2014 syllabuses will take into account the ideas in the REC's non-statutory Framework from 2013.[9]

Some points to note:

 Agreed syllabuses are reviewed every five years, so you might bear this in mind when putting together your school or departmental improvement plan for RE – don't do lots of development work just before a new syllabus comes out! You might consider getting involved

---

[5] School Standards and Framework Act 1998, Schedule 19; Education Act 2002, Section 80.

[6] The Education (Special Educational Needs) (England) (Consolidation) (Amendment) Regulations 2006 Regulation 5A.

[7] Education Act 1996 Schedule 31.

[8] Education Act 1996 Section 375.

[9] *A Curriculum Framework for Religious Education in England* (REC 2013).

in the process of reviewing the syllabus and get in touch with your local SACRE. If you are an academy or free school, you might also consider a review cycle of five years, in order to keep your curriculum up to date.

② **It is important not to confuse legislation regarding RE with that of collective worship**. In England there should be daily acts of 'collective worship', a majority of which should be 'wholly or mainly of a broadly Christian character' and should take account of the ages and backgrounds of the pupils involved. In Scotland a 'regular' act of 'religious observance' is required. RE and collective worship have obvious areas of overlap and commonality, and can be mutually supportive of each other, but they are not the same in law.

③ **Right of withdrawal.** This was first granted when RE was actually religious *instruction* and carried with it connotations of induction into the Christian faith. RE is very different now – open, broad, exploring a range of religious and non-religious worldviews. However, in the UK, parents still have the right to withdraw their children from RE/RME (Religious and Moral Education, in Scotland) on the grounds that they wish to provide their own religious education.[10] This will be the parents' responsibility. However, it is good practice to talk to parents to ensure that they understand the aims and value of RE/RME before honouring this right.

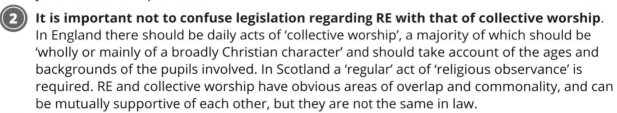

RE around the UK

Northern Ireland

RE is a statutory subject of the school curriculum between Foundation Stage and Key Stage 4. The Core Syllabus determines RE content for all grant-aided schools, drawn up by the four Christian churches of Northern Ireland and the Department for Education. Based on this, schools can develop a programme of RE that suits their particular needs.

The Core Syllabus contains a requirement for world religions to be studied. At Key Stage 4 students learn about the Christian Church from both a Protestant and Catholic perspective.

Scotland

Religious and Moral Education (RME) is a statutory subject of the Scottish 3–18 curriculum, which relates to schools but not pre-school centres. RME encompasses two dimensions: that relating to non-denominational and that relating to Catholic schools (RERC – Religious Education in Roman Catholic schools). In non-denominational schools the RME curriculum will offer an understanding of Christianity but will also take account of the local context. In Catholic schools it is acknowledged that RERC will be part of supporting Catholic children in their faith development.

Wales

RE is a statutory subject in the Welsh 3–19 curriculum. The RE curriculum will be derived from the locally agreed syllabus determined by the local SACRE. The RE curriculum will reflect the fact that Christianity as well as the principal religions represented in Britain should be studied at each key stage.

Although RE in Wales is non-denominational, teaching *about* a particular catechism or denomination is acceptable for the sake of comparison and understanding.

---

[10] School Standards and Framework Act 1998, S71 (3).

What is the Framework?

In 2011 the Department for Education (DfE) announced a review of the National Curriculum. However, it left out RE. In a bid to remain in line with national developments, the REC funded a thorough review of both the subject and the curriculum, resulting in the 2013 *Review of Religious Education in England*, which includes a re-fashioned RE Curriculum Framework.

Do I have to follow the Framework?

No – this is non-statutory guidance. The legal requirement to follow a locally agreed syllabus (or trust deeds, faith community guidelines or academy syllabus) has not changed (see pp.4–5).

What is it for, then?

There is no National Curriculum for RE, but the 2013 Curriculum Framework offers national guidance for the development of locally agreed syllabuses and for the RE curriculum in academies and free schools. The review of RE and the curriculum it contains represents an articulation of current thinking about the aims and purposes of RE and has been developed through wide consultation. At a time when all National Curriculum subjects have been overhauled, the Framework was produced to support RE in schools, and to encourage the development of the subject.

What does the Framework offer?

1. **Clarity on aims and purposes:** After wide consultation it was found that the aims and purposes of RE were not always well understood and agreed syllabuses across the country varied in quality. The Framework sets out the purpose of study and aims of RE (see p.3). These mark out the field of study for RE, with a clear focus on knowledge and skills concerning understanding religious and non-religious worldviews, as well as developing pupils' own abilities to engage in thinking and talking about matters to do with religion and belief.

2. **A vision of high-quality RE:** The REC review notes that RE can be of high quality when it is well taught. One aim of the Curriculum Framework is to articulate the kind of high-quality RE that inspires pupils, to help teachers appreciate what to aim for in their classrooms. The emphasis is on high standards and coherence in what is taught. The Framework does not give detailed content but leaves space for teachers to use their own professionalism and expertise to enable pupils to realise their potential.

3. **A basis for planning an RE curriculum:** The Framework is designed to provide a basis for SACREs to develop a syllabus and to help academies and free schools who do not have to use the locally agreed syllabus. The Framework is written to support all types of schools and provide national guidance.

4. **Curriculum continuity (11–14s):** The REC review recommends that education policy should 'promote coherence and progression between 4–14 programmes of study and 14–19 public examinations'.[11] This recommendation reflects an awareness that the requirements of the GCSE exam have a distorting effect on 11–14 RE. This is partly due to the skills required at GCSE, which feed down into the 11–14 curriculum. However, this recommendation was concerned with the effect of the popular philosophy and ethics units at GCSE, which have decreased the amount of specifically religious content covered. This recommendation seeks to reinstate the deep, demanding and detailed study of religions themselves for 11–14s, in order that 'religious education' is indeed an education about matters of religion. Revision of the criteria for GCSE specifications in England in 2015 has also addressed this lack of focus on religion.

---

[11] *A Review of Religious Education in England* (REC 2013), p.32.

Clarity on outcomes in RE: The Framework sets out how RE can enable high-quality learning by establishing outcomes for ages 7, 11 and 14 related to the threefold aims of RE (see p.3). These are clarified by, and illustrated with, examples of the kinds of activities that might lead pupils to achieving an outcome.

For example, outcome A3 for 11-year-olds says that pupils should be taught to 'Explore and describe a range of beliefs, symbols and actions so that they can understand different ways of life and ways of expressing meaning.'[12]

The guidance examples given to clarify this include:

- Pupils pursue an enquiry into beliefs about worship, relating the meanings of symbols and actions used in worship such as bowing down, making music together, sharing food or speaking to God (e.g. in prayer) to events and teachings from a religion they study.
- Pupils consider how the meanings of a parable of Jesus are expressed in poetry, video, stained glass and drama.
- Pupils describe the impact of Hindu teaching about harmlessness (ahimsa) on questions about what people eat and how people treat animals. They express their own ideas.[13]

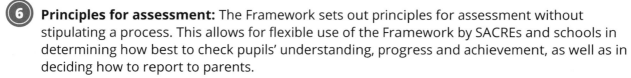 **Principles for assessment:** The Framework sets out principles for assessment without stipulating a process. This allows for flexible use of the Framework by SACREs and schools in determining how best to check pupils' understanding, progress and achievement, as well as in deciding how to report to parents.

What are the most significant changes to look out for?

1 The Framework uses the term 'worldviews' to refer to non-religious beliefs and traditions, such as Humanism.

2 The Framework says that pupils should develop a systematic knowledge and understanding of religions and non-religious worldviews. This seems to imply less emphasis on thematic teaching, but need not. It does mean that syllabuses and school curricula should be careful to ensure that both systematic and thematic teaching provide a coherent encounter with religions and worldviews across the age range. It also implies that depth is preferable to breadth, and therefore that agreed syllabuses should be realistic about how many religions can reasonably be studied in a key stage.

3 The commonly used attainment targets from 2004, 'learning about religion' and 'learning from religion', have lost their prominence, although they can still be discerned within the Framework. This is because there is evidence that schools were divorcing these two perspectives in RE, with a reduction in teaching quality, pupil experience and achievement as a result. The Framework aims seek to develop a coherent and integrated RE.

4 The Framework does not set out level statements for assessment and attainment. It will be for SACREs and individual schools to develop assessment processes.

---

[12] *A Curriculum Framework for Religious Education in England* (REC 2013), p.18.
[13] Ibid.

Get the vision!

As RE subject leader, one of your most important roles is to articulate a shared vision of RE in your school. Ideally, this will be arrived at through conversation with other teachers and senior leaders. Consider what RE in your school is for. What do you want pupils to know and be able to do? What do your pupils in their particular local context *need* to know and be able to do as they grow? What learning skills and personal characteristics will you promote? Look at the aims and purposes of RE on pages 2–3 to help in your considerations.

Construct a curriculum

Hand in hand with your vision for RE is what will be taught. Each unit of work in each age group should be planned to reflect your shared view of the purpose of RE in your school. Your curriculum will be based on your locally agreed syllabus or faith community guidelines, or, if you are an academy or free school, you may develop your own (see pp.2–3 for details about this and pp.6–7 for an outline of how the non-statutory national 2013 Framework for RE can help in developing a curriculum).

The curriculum needs to be balanced and coherent, enabling pupils to have appropriate encounters with a range of religions and worldviews through the age ranges, building on prior learning and making suitable progress in understanding and skills.

You will need to consider which religions are taught and when, taking into consideration the school and local community as well as wider national and global perspectives. Many people recommend that depth is better than breadth in terms of pupils' understanding and religious literacy.

Focus on teaching and learning

Your school will have policies and practices to do with teaching and learning, and you should be clear that RE teaching needs to be of high quality. Planning and assessment procedures should be understood and followed by all teachers. Lessons should be well planned, engaging pupils in an encounter with religion and belief as living realities, connecting where appropriate with pupils' own experience and understanding, but necessarily extending their experience and understanding.

Plan for progress

As a subject leader you should not be planning every single RE lesson taught in your school, but you will have overall responsibility for the RE curriculum and schemes of work. Being clear about what you want pupils to know and be able to do at the end of each lesson or series of lessons is important, as this then enables you to devise multiple ways of helping pupils to achieve a goal. Sometimes RE can be a marvellously unexpected journey of discovery for pupils, but this is usually a product of excellent planning! Make sure that assessment is integrated within planning.

There is more information about planning and assessment below (see pp.16–17 and 57–75).

Know what is happening

Regular discussion and sharing of your own and colleagues' marking, planning and their pupils' progress enables you to offer support where necessary and to celebrate excellent practice. It will also inform your ongoing understanding of the development of RE in your school. It will encourage the development of a mutually supportive team and keep the focus firmly on the experience and development of pupils. Regularly visit each other's classrooms for supportive, focused observations, asking questions such as:

- Do I enable all pupils to participate?
- How helpful are my questions? Do they help me to identify misconceptions?
- How well do my activities develop the understanding of boys or girls or SEN pupils?
- How well do I enable progress?

This will acclimatise you to observations without the pressures of inspection!

Keep on growing!

Even the most expert RE teachers and subject leaders benefit from continuing professional development (CPD). For teachers with more limited specialist training, RE-specific professional development can boost confidence, increase subject knowledge and inspire greater creativity and commitment. Research suggests that the minimum time for effective CPD is 15 hours,[14] sustained over at least two terms with time for teachers to apply and implement their learning. It is worth it!

Raise the status of RE in your school

Make the most of opportunities to represent the nature, value and purpose of RE to pupils, parents, colleagues, school leaders and governors. For example:

- Create a buzz in your classroom, the corridors, assemblies, at open evenings and on RE days.
- Create eye-catching, exciting displays that tell the pupils clearly what sort of subject they are dealing with.
- Celebrate excellent RE work, articulating clearly why the work is high quality, and make a splash when giving out awards, certificates or prizes.
- Invite other subject specialists into your lessons to take part in discussions relevant to their areas of expertise. Show that RE has wide relevance and contains many other disciplines such as history, poetry, art, music and so on.
- Create a pupil forum for RE. Allow pupils to be genuinely involved in planning and delivering aspects of RE, such as choosing discussion topics, planning a contribution to an assembly and teaching parts of lessons.
- Offer taster lessons after school for parents. Show them how much RE has changed since they were at school!
- Send excellent RE work to school leaders with the expectation that they will praise the pupils.
- Object if pupils are removed by the school from RE for spurious reasons (such as needing more time on English or Maths – they already have many, many more hours than you!). You may find you only have to object once or twice before the message gets through.

Networking

Being an RE subject leader can be a lonely experience. Become a member of NATRE and receive termly advice and inspiration as well as monthly downloads and offers on webinars and national conferences. Join (or start) a NATRE-affiliated local group to meet other teachers, share ideas and support each other. These are great ways to feel connected and inspired and to help you make the most of your valuable and influential role.

Useful links

- Guidance on RE subject leadership: www.reonline.org.uk/leading
- National Society 'Statement of Entitlement for RE' in Church of England schools bit.ly/1pUBpqV
- See the REC's CPD portal for information about what training is available: www.theredirectory.org.uk/pdportal; also consult RE Today's training web page: www.retoday.org.uk/courses
- Self-evaluation in RE: rehandbook.org.uk/section/managing/self-evaluation-in-re
- RE Quality Mark: www.reqm.org. Aim high, go for gold – use this to develop RE in your school!

---

[14] Robert Coe, *Improving Education* (Centre of Education and Monitoring 2013), p.xiv. www.cem.org/attachments/publications/ImprovingEducation2013.pdf

Context

A major challenge for the subject leader in primary schools today is that of enabling colleagues with other specialisms and priorities to do a good job in RE, and with enthusiasm and integrity. Similarly, in secondary schools the head of RE often leads a team of colleagues with other specialisms. In RE, perhaps more than in other subjects, this can be compounded by the different approaches to the subject among a staff team.

Some teachers have a great commitment to and interest in teaching their own faith or belief, but not other faiths. Some teachers question the place of RE in the curriculum, often because they misunderstand the educational rationale for the subject. Sometimes they felt indoctrinated during their own experience of RE. Some teachers may exercise their right to opt out of RE teaching on grounds of conscience.

Often the priorities of teachers are so many that RE will not be top of the list for long. This is quite reasonable, and it means that when the subject is considered, e.g. once a term at a primary staff meeting or through an annual CPD opportunity, the quality of input needs to be good and the agenda needs to move forward rather than chewing over old questions.

The issue of confidence is perhaps the most crucial. Many excellent teachers feel so lacking in confidence in a subject where many different religions offer different solutions to life's uncertain riddles that their RE work is confined to telling stories, 'doing' festivals or discussing vaguely ethical stories from the newspapers.

Team leaders need to find ways of building the confidence of colleagues so that more imaginative teaching and learning strategies can be developed. Such confidence grows where people can find a little time and space to share their concerns and to have them addressed.

Strategies to build up successful RE teams

The subject leader needs to develop strategies such as the following to build up the team's understanding of RE and each teacher's confidence to deliver the subject well:

- ways of addressing people's reasonable concerns about aims in RE
- a clearly structured policy statement, devised by all those involved, and widely understood
- schemes of work that are easy to use, practical and comprehensive
- clarity about the outcomes of RE work by pupils in different age groups: examples of a range of pupils' achievements and clear reference to the assessment structures of your syllabus or school
- support with subject knowledge, so that teachers can feel confident with the material they are teaching
- team planning that involves everybody from the start, though the subject leader will provide support and direction
- well-thought-out and varied resources, stored in usable ways
- support for teachers where they lack confidence (conversation, teacher observation, books to refer to, access to training and other kinds of support)
- openness about how to handle the teacher's own beliefs and assumptions in the classroom
- agreement about the time that is spent on RE in the classroom
- monitoring of pupils' work in RE (to avoid 'ten in the bed' syndrome, where one subject 'falls out' – it's always RE!).

TWOS in RE

RE is more often taught by 'Teachers With Other Specialisms' (TWOS) than almost any other subject. While this is not an ideal situation, many TWOS bring their gifts as teachers to the subject, including expertise in particular parts of the RE field: e.g. historians may be good at teaching interpretation, drama teachers at engaging pupils with issues, and science teachers in tackling empirical approaches to religion.

- The first need for TWOS is to find and assimilate a professional rationale for their RE work. This won't happen without training and time to think about what the subject is for.

- Research emphasises that subject expertise has a significant impact upon pupil outcomes in the classroom, so support with subject knowledge will be vital at all phases.

- RE teaching deserves to be planned on the same basis as teaching other subjects. If there is a long-term need to use staff without training, the minimum satisfactory approach involves continuity of deployment and appropriate professional development for those involved.

- RE should not be taught by the unwilling or the press-ganged. This is unfair on teachers and pupils and is unprofessional.

Questions for RE team leaders

- In what ways have you been successful in building your RE team? What factors have enabled this success?

- What are the most difficult aspects of building a team for RE teaching in your school? To whom can you talk about addressing these problems?

- What do you see as the next steps forward in building more successful RE across the team? How can these be monitored?

Using TWOS can be successful, but can also contribute to low standards. Careful and supportive monitoring and intervention to change and improve the quality of teaching is the key to success.

Are you a teacher with another specialism, teaching RE?

As a TWOS, you can enjoy teaching RE and bring to your lessons a variety of teaching backgrounds and curriculum expertise. TWOS can make natural links with other areas of the curriculum that broaden and deepen the pupils' understanding of RE. Good practice shared is a powerful tool for raising standards and you should not be afraid of using learning approaches you employ for other subject areas in helping pupils achieve the learning outcomes.

Six tips for surviving (and flourishing)

1 You won't know all the answers; specialists don't either! Own up when you are stuck, say that you will find out – or set pupils the challenge of finding out.

2 Be clear about what you want pupils to achieve, but remember that occasional diversions into ultimate questions or questions of meaning can prompt some important insights, as well as develop pupils' thinking, listening and communication skills.

3 Be careful of the language you use. As RE teachers, we need to be as open and objective as possible, whilst acknowledging our biases. Bear in mind that no one is actually objective in this subject. There are different schools of thought about how much you reveal about your own views, but be warned that the pupils will question you whichever path you take.

4 Be careful not to imply that all believers in a tradition think the same way. You may try to say something like 'Some Christians believe … whilst others believe …' Some regard this as a little simplistic, but it helps pupils to appreciate the diversity that exists within as well as between faith traditions and communities.

5 Try to be consistent with technical language, but recognise that there are often different spellings of translated words. Accuracy is helpful, but not at the expense of understanding the meaning and significance of the words within a tradition. (See pages 81–112) for more information.)

6 RE is a subject where there can be legitimate connections with pupils' own experience, whether personal (e.g. their experience of commitment) or through national or world events (e.g. ethical questions raised in the media or through TV soaps). Making links can help pupils to see the relevance of the subject to life. Remember that we need to take pupils beyond their own experience too!

Supporting the subject: how can I build up the status of RE?

This page will help you think about how to build the status of RE in your school through a checklist of questions. While the list is aspirational, each of these things can be changed and improved with careful good practice.

You could use the list for development planning (to assess and set targets to develop your school's RE). You could send your filled-in copy to school leaders and governors to ensure RE is supported in your school. The list of practical suggestions offers a starting point for getting the school buzzing with your RE!

	Fully	Partially	Not at all
Are all legal requirements for the subject met?			
Is there a proper job description for the subject leader, with appropriate remuneration (as for other subjects)?			
Is RE provision recognised as good quality internally (e.g. by governors) and externally (e.g. by inspectors)? If not, are there any realistic plans to change and improve?			
Does the RE subject leader get a fair chance to contribute to whole-school curriculum and assessment decisions and policies? Are the particular contributions of the subject recognised and well developed?			
Does the school recognise the contribution of RE to whole-school requirements such as spiritual, moral, social and cultural development, the promotion of 'British values' and pupils' well-being?			
Are pupils' questions about 'why we do RE' answered to their satisfaction?			
What do pupils say about their RE? Is it challenging, interesting, provocative, something they are proud of? If you don't know, run a questionnaire activity to find out.			
Is the range of teaching and learning in RE broad and deep, enabling achievement for all?			
Is curriculum time adequate? Is it broadly similar to other curriculum areas such as History, Geography, Music or Art?			
Are financial resources adequate – broadly similar to History, Geography, Art or Music?			
Do pupils have entitlement to go on an RE educational visit?			
Can parents see that RE is a valuable part of their child's education?			
Does reporting and achievement in RE match structures for the foundation subjects?			
Is the work of the teaching team monitored as it is in other areas of the curriculum, e.g. literacy?			
Is there support, professional development and practical day-to-day help for teachers with other specialisms who work in RE?			
Does the subject leader have time to manage the teaching team?			
Is the deployment of staff to RE classes effective and comparable to other subjects?			
Is there a forum for the celebration of excellence in pupils' RE work?			
Is the RE subject leader aware of any hostility to RE, based on misunderstanding among staff, parents or pupils? Is it addressed?			
In conclusion, is the 'playing field' of curriculum decision-making level?			

A school policy statement for RE: what does one look like?

Schools need an RE policy statement that accurately describes actual practice in RE and which also:

- sets out clearly the rationale, aims and objectives
- provides all teachers with a framework
- informs parents and inspectors about the RE curriculum within the school.

Many schools will have a standard framework for curriculum policy statements. To adapt such a framework to meet the requirements of RE, you should include the following:

1 Legal requirements and time allocation for RE

- making it clear that RE is distinct from collective worship, which is not counted as curriculum time

2 A statement about the place of RE in the curriculum

- an important opportunity to explain the valuable contribution RE makes to pupils' development and to help colleagues understand what RE is and is not!

3 The purpose and aims of RE

- based on the syllabus (e.g. agreed syllabus) but indicating school priorities

4 Content and approach

- religions taught
- approach to teaching religions: thematic, by religion or a mixture of both, with a rationale for the approach taken

5 Scheme of work outline

- an overview of teaching units for each phase or key stage

6 Methodology

- how RE is taught: an outline of teaching and learning strategies encouraged and used
- reference to the development of skills and attitudes

7 Resources

- books, artefacts, videos, ICT hardware and software, local resource centre address, local contacts

8 Assessment

- a brief statement summarising how the school makes use of, for example, intended learning outcomes and end-of-key stage statements to recognise and report on pupils' progress in RE

RE and other aspects of the curriculum

- spiritual, moral, social and cultural development of pupils: British values; a statement of the specific contribution RE makes to pupils' development in these areas, with examples of current practice
- inclusion: a sentence summarising the school's commitment to valuing the opinions, beliefs and practices of all, and handling minority groups and opinions with sensitivity; a statement about provision for pupils in RE with a range of needs including those with special educational needs and those who are gifted or talented

 Withdrawal

- a statement of the rights of parents to withdraw their children from RE, expressed in a way that demonstrates the school's positive attitude to RE and the benefits it brings to pupils

Further references

- syllabus details (e.g. agreed syllabus, examination specifications, trust deed).

Planning any subject is vital. Investing precious time in planning has many benefits for teachers and pupils. Planning:

- ensures pupils encounter a coherent programme of learning that takes into account, where appropriate, learning in other subjects. This is especially true in primary schools
- allows for pupil progress in knowledge, understanding and skills as pupils engage with a planned programme of learning
- should be a shared process, drawing on the expertise of everyone, giving a sense of ownership and encouraging enthusiasm and teamwork.

In school there are three levels of planning that organise the teaching and learning pupils will undertake in their RE lessons:

- long-term planning (key stage overview)
- medium-term planning (units of work or investigations)
- short-term planning (lessons).

Long-term planning: the key stage overview

Who? Subject leader (RE co-ordinator or head of department), although ideally involving all teachers of RE in your school.

What? Use the programme of study from the agreed syllabus, faith community guidelines or the RE curriculum that is the appropriate document for your school type (see p.4). Organise the programme of study across the key stage to ensure the requirements are met.

Remember: You should be able to provide a rationale for the way you have organised the RE curriculum, enabling a coherent approach to religions and religion, through systematic and thematic units. Look for connections with other subjects where appropriate.

Medium-term planning: planning units of work or investigations

Who? Teachers working in close consultation with the subject leader. Teachers may need support as they undertake this process.

What? These plans should give detail on the unit key question, learning outcomes, assessment, subject content, and suggested teaching and learning activities designed to meet the requirements of the long-term plan and appropriate programme of study.

Remember: Medium-term planning must clearly show learning outcomes and essential subject content. Other parts of the planning are designed to be adapted as you teach each class.

Short-term planning: lesson planning

Who? The class teacher.

What? A clear plan of what will be done in the lesson to enable the intended learning outcomes to be achieved, taking into account the different needs of the pupils.

Remember: Use a variety of teaching and learning strategies to engage, enthuse and stretch pupils.

Three levels of curriculum planning: some points to consider

When writing long-term plans ensure that you:

- meet statutory requirements (e.g. using your agreed syllabus, diocesan or faith community guidelines, the non-statutory 2013 Framework or Scottish Curriculum for Excellence)

- select or follow the guidance on which religions and worldviews are to be taught in each key stage and year group
- create the opportunity for pupils to gain a systematic understanding of religion (e.g. by writing key questions that look at one religion only as well as units that follow a theme)
- organise how the programme of study is to be divided up across the years within each key stage
- consider how much time is needed for each unit to be studied and whether this is to be through weekly lessons or blocked time, where this is possible
- ensure continuity and progression in knowledge and understanding in the religions and worldviews taught – make sure units build on prior learning; ask yourself why pupils are encountering this unit at this point
- liaise with other staff and consider what is taught in other subjects in order to take advantage of opportunities to link learning (e.g. a shared visit or links between subjects)
- audit existing resources against the scheme of work; determine any deficiencies and make provision for resource development for RE
- consider staff development needs – could someone go on a course and feed back ideas?

When writing medium-term plans, ensure that you:
- consider the excellent practice of formulating unit plans or investigations around questions
- start with a key question or area that you want to investigate with the pupils
- clearly relate this question to the long-term plan and build on prior learning
- start with a question devised by the teacher and give pupils opportunity to add any questions they are interested in exploring (keep the questions relevant to your long-term plan and dealing with religion and belief)
- are clear about the subject knowledge or content that the key question will address; how far will your key question open up this area?
- write clear key learning outcomes: what do you want the pupils to be able to know, understand and do as a result of the unit of learning?
- assess: this does not always need to be formal, but within the unit you will look at a piece or pieces of work in more detail to capture progress and write a range and sequence of teaching and learning activities, bearing in mind that engaged pupils are usually more effective learners!

When writing short-term plans ensure that you:
- are very clear about what pupils already know and understand: without this step, further learning can be fatally undermined!
- are clear about what you are aiming to achieve: the learning outcome for the lesson
- are confident about the subject content of the lesson and that the lesson meets the needs of all pupils
- are able to give feedback on pupil progress, showing them clear next steps for learning
- are able to utilise current events and active learning strategies to engage their learning
- are prepared to step off the plan if a fruitful avenue opens up within a lesson.

Creative curriculum planning

RE must be planned for high standards, but there is not a 'one-size-fits-all' approach. All pupils, aged 4–19, are entitled to high-quality learning in RE, so schools must plan sufficient time for the subject to be well taught. There is no legal requirement for a set amount of time for RE, but the long-standing recommendation in England is a minimum of:

4–5s	36 hours per year (equivalent to 1 hour per week)
5–7s	36 hours per year
7–11s	45 hours per year (equivalent to 75 minutes per week)
11–14s	45 hours per year
14–16s	40 hours per year (5% curriculum time) for pupils not following an examination course; full course GCSE in England requires equivalent time to other GCSE subjects
16–19s	recommendations vary

Subject leaders for RE, heads of department, senior staff, headteachers and governors all contribute to ensuring provision promotes and enables the highest standards. Governors are ultimately responsible for providing a curriculum that supports pupils in reaching the standards set out in the agreed syllabus or guidelines a school follows.

Options for organising RE time

Discrete teaching of RE: Many schools use one or two weekly lessons of RE as the standard way of designing the curriculum. The advantages of this are that pupils get used to the RE lesson, the progress they make can be steady and continuous, and teachers 'know where they are'. Some primary schools have trained specialist RE teachers who take discrete RE lessons across the school. These teachers can become real experts and advocates for the subject, but the rest of the teaching staff quickly become de-skilled. The main disadvantage is that pupils' weekly experience of RE can be too spread out for the deeper learning that the subject requires to flourish. RE can sometimes be squeezed out of the weekly primary timetable by other curriculum pressures.

Blocked themed teaching: Some schools use a themed approach to the curriculum and RE becomes part of this. A series of lessons in the humanities or other subjects are themed with a relevant focus for RE, for a fixed period of time, and determined by the outcomes to be delivered. Blocked learning can last for two weeks or for longer – for example for half a term – and pupils spend five hours a week or more learning RE and relating study to History or Geography. In the next half-term, the focus may be more on one of the other subjects.

The main advantages of this approach are that pupils get a deeper and more continuous experience of RE. Working in depth allows children the time they need to consolidate their learning. A disadvantage is that some schools use arbitrary themes, with little or no substantial link to RE, or fail to plan RE into the programme at sufficient depth.

If RE is linked with other subjects in this blocked-time approach, you should ensure that RE has the opportunity to be the lead area where appropriate. Do not allow RE to be shoe-horned in just to tick a box: RE does not have to fit every themed unit, so look for balance across the year.

A suggested model: 'Big RE' days and weeks

Some schools use an 'RE week' or an 'RE day' to focus learning, then follow up the 'big experience' with linked lessons over several weeks. Such 'big events' planning is demanding of teachers, but can help the whole school to focus on and develop the subject.

A day is about five hours, so is not, of course, a substitute for a term's work! It is not sufficient to replace weekly RE with a couple of RE days a year – this is weak provision and will set low standards. RE days are an enhancement of regular provision. RE weeks can, with careful organisation, be a way of teaching a substantial part of the RE curriculum, but they need to be

regular and committed to RE. Some schools have six RE weeks per year and ensure that 8–10 hours of those weeks focus on RE. Best practice ensures that there is ongoing assessment of pupils' understanding, and that the weeks build on prior learning and are part of a coherent long-term plan (see pp.16–17). The keys to successful RE days and weeks are clarity about the planned RE learning, and ensuring that the learning is achieved.

Here are some suggestions for 'Big RE' themes.

1 Inspirational leaders: choose your hero
A day to focus on Jesus or the Prophet Muhammad, Gandhi, Revd Dr Martin Luther King, Jackie Pullinger, Mother Teresa or Aung San Suu Kyi, asking pupils: Whom do you most admire and why? Mix discovery, biography, movie clips and dilemmas with young people's own ideas, reactions and views. At the end of the day, pupils 'build their own religious/spiritual superhero for the twenty-first century', bringing their ideas together in craft and writing.

2 An Easter week: what's so important about Easter for Christians?
A week to bring together learning about Jesus, exploring the events of Holy Week in creative and experiential ways, but importantly to explore the significance of Easter for Christians, getting to grips with key concepts like incarnation, sacrifice, salvation and resurrection. Where does Easter fit in to the bigger story of the Bible? Bring some Christian visitors into school to be grilled about what difference Easter makes to their lives!

3 Debating hot topics
Pupils research and discover more about religious practice in a range of faiths, presenting their findings to each other. Use methods like P4C (Philosophy for Children) to explore big questions with pupils early in the week so that they can run a really exciting and well-thought-out, formal debate that involves everyone later in the week. Topics could include: Does prayer work? Why do people suffer? Would the world be better with more religion or less? Why are some people very religious, but others not at all? What will make our town a more respectful place?

4 Global citizenship
Exploring the problems of inequality and poverty, and finding out how charities like Islamic Relief, Sewa International or Christian Aid act out their faith and make a difference for those whose lives are damaged by HIV/AIDS, war, famine or big business. Pupils take part in role play to decide how a charity should use its funds and consider: Who in our class is going to change the world? How? Why? What makes one person able to make a difference in a world of need?

For more ideas on planning for 'Big RE', see Lat Blaylock, Fiona Moss and Stephen Pett, *Big RE: Enriching RE through an RE Day or an RE Week* (RE Today 2013).

Creative curriculum planning can present both opportunities and challenges for RE: are all staff confident to teach? Why do inspectors sometimes find RE is least well covered in an integrated programme of learning? Do some themes enable RE effectively, but others exclude RE? Schools must consider the programme of study within the syllabus and teaching arrangements in other subjects in deciding whether RE learning is well served by 'creative curriculum planning'.

In deciding the ways in which the programme of study will be implemented, schools owe it to their pupils to ensure that the full range of RE opportunities is offered to all.

Inclusion refers to the right of every child to access a stimulating and useful curriculum whatever their ability and background and even if they are experiencing difficulties in their lives. Many groups of young people are at risk of educational exclusion, such as:

- pupils for whom English is an additional language (EAL)
- migrant children, such as travellers, asylum seekers and recent immigrants
- children with Special Educational Needs (SEN), which could be cognitive, physical, behavioural or a combination
- children who, for a variety of reasons, display behavioural, emotional or social difficulties (BESD)
- 'looked after' children who are in the care of the local council
- children and young people who are carers
- girls and young women who are pregnant
- young people who are ill or who suffer mental health problems
- young people who are exposed to violence, crime or substance abuse in their home environment
- gifted and talented pupils who are not stretched and challenged.

However, all children learn differently and will respond to different activities and teaching styles. This may be due to their gender, interests, natural talents or background. In a wider sense, inclusion describes a teacher's responsibility to differentiate according to his or her pupils' needs, to ensure equal opportunities for achievement and success.

While inclusion is a statutory duty across all subjects, RE teachers have many opportunities to model an inclusive classroom, showing pupils that everyone has the right to be heard and taken seriously. RE can boost pupils' self-esteem by confirming that their views are important and offering a safe space to share their doubts and hopes.

Pupils with SEN

In special schools

Pupils with learning difficulties in special schools, working with teachers who understand their particular needs and strengths, should be enabled to access the meaningful concepts underlying RE topics, as well as offered the opportunity to express their own ideas, thoughts and feelings.

In mainstream schools

Pupils with learning difficulties in mainstream schools need:

- work that is manageable in small steps, but, wherever possible, not 'dumbed down'
- work that allows them to access the deeper concepts that give RE topics meaning
- to see the relevance, value and importance of what they learn
- to understand how to make progress
- to experience a range of learning approaches, including opportunities to express their thoughts and feelings
- to be praised and encouraged appropriately.

The ideas below were developed at a special school by an RE specialist, but could be adapted to the mainstream classroom.

Strategies for SEN pupils in the mainstream classroom

Anne Krisman, a specialist RE teacher at Little Heath School, a special school for pupils with moderate to severe learning difficulties, has developed the 'Five Keys into RE' approach for pupils with SEN. It can be adapted for the mainstream school classroom.[15]

---

[15] We are very grateful to Anne for her permission to relay her innovative ideas. Find out more in the Ofsted 'Best Practice' case study here: bit.ly/1J6XDzY. Find more ideas from Anne Krisman on the Five Keys approach here: www.reonline.org.uk/supporting/re-matters/news-inner/?id=15291.

At the heart of Anne Krisman's work is the need to unlock the core concepts of religion and spirituality in a way that makes sense to young people with special needs, starting with how they see themselves, their lives and the world around them. Religion has much to say about the spiritual experience of being human and experiencing sadness, loss, love and hope. This means that bringing these ancient stores of wisdom to the classroom, rather than simply transferring factual knowledge, is much more valuable for students with SEN. Experiential learning needs to be part of a connected thread of meaning that links a religion's deep theology of humanity with the pupils' lives.

1. **Connection** – make links between the pupils' lives and the meaning of a religious story or concept to enable the fullest understanding. For example, reflecting on the pupils' own experiences of seeing their loved ones again after a period of separation could unlock the story of Rama and Sita or the Prodigal Son, encouraging engagement with the universal human story beneath.

2. **Knowledge** – abandon all extraneous information and focus on the 'burning core' at the centre of the topic. What is meaningful to the pupils? Let them explore this rather than focusing on content that does not relate to their lives. If they take longer to come to an understanding, make sure they are exploring the most interesting element.

3. **Senses** – maximise chances for them to taste, feel and hold artefacts, as pupils with SEN will learn through their senses more than through abstract thinking. However, ensure these artefacts are pertinent to the lesson's overall theme and contribute to meaning rather than detract or distract from it. Music is very powerful: chants, authentic prayers and devotional music can convey the intensity of religious traditions and of a believer's experiences.

4. **Symbols** – these are accessible ways into deeper meaning developed by religious traditions for the sake of understanding, so use them! Religious art, sculpture, architecture, precious objects and symbols are pathways to lead a person into the deeper meaning of a theme.

5. **Values** – identify the values underpinning the religious theme and make them explicit. Young people with SEN are as awake to values as any young person and therefore ideas such as helping others, saying sorry and treating people fairly are enormously meaningful. They link to the pupils' own lives and values and bring the religious theme more fully to life.

'Gifted and talented': challenging the most able pupils in RE

Medium-term plans or individual lessons should be created with an outcome in mind (see pp.16–17) – what do you want your pupils to know and be able to do by the end of the unit or the end of the lesson? This planning process is incredibly important when you want to stretch and stimulate your most able pupils. Make sure you have opportunities not just for recalling and describing factual content, but interpreting, interrogating and critiquing. A good place to start is with each lesson's key question. The question 'Why is Jesus' death important to Christians?' could be re-phrased as 'Would Christianity be the same if Jesus hadn't died?' in order to offer opportunities for a much deeper level of analysis and evaluation. The re-phrased question should not require more content, but offer greater opportunities for pupils to debate a meaty issue, which, if planned well, requires less input from the teacher and more from the pupils!

When planning challenging RE ...

- At the point in learning when you stop to consolidate, make sure you have planned some analysis or interpretation questions as well as comprehension. For example, instead of 'Why do Muslims give zakat?' ask 'Can you be a Muslim if you don't give zakat?'

- Assessment for learning will be ongoing, but when preparing pupils for specific assessment tasks, start with the outcomes or mark scheme and make it clear how the highest marks or grades are to be earned.

- Make sure pupils have enough factual knowledge and a stretching question when preparing to evaluate. Feed their brains with relevant information that they must use in their comments and arguments rather than accepting their own unsupported opinion.

- Know your lesson outcomes and critical question and direct the discussion to that end rather than letting it ramble in any direction. Push pupils for further clarification if you think they are articulating an important concept and ask other pupils to comment on what has been said. Keep control of the discussion with the learning aims in mind.

- Articulate for the whole class why a pupil's answer was high quality: 'Sam has made a clear link between what a Muslim believes about God and why Muslims pray'; 'Jay used the passage from Genesis to explain why Christians support the sanctity of life'; or 'Aisha, you have justified your argument, and that means I can see why you have come to your conclusion.'

- Give out red, orange and green cards. Pupils must offer a negative view (red), a positive view (green) or a view that moves the conversation along (orange). You might challenge them to do this in order to leave the lesson at break time (or the end of the lesson in secondary schools). This sets the expectation that all pupils will be engaged and thinking throughout the lesson.

- Ask for feedback regularly in quick and unobtrusive ways. This could be a simple show of hands ('Who thinks Jo's description included the most important parts?' 'Who thought Maya made a reasonable point? Who is not convinced?'), sharing some thoughts with a neighbour for a couple of minutes or writing 20 words in response to a short question. You can call upon pupils to explain themselves, or not, as you wish, but again this gives the constant expectation that pupils will be engaged and thinking for themselves.

- Play little games using keywords or key facts; design shorts tests of key vocabulary or plenaries testing factual knowledge. Set the expectation that factual knowledge is the basis of good evaluation and pupils need to learn it.

- If you can't answer a question or a pupil has caught you out in discussion, don't be afraid to show it! Take the class with you as you find out the answer or grapple with an argument. The class will learn from your approach of humility and willingness to learn, even if it means admitting you are wrong from time to time. They will learn more than they ever could from a book.

Supporting behaviour through RE

Young people who display challenging behaviour, whether in a Pupil Referral Unit or mainstream school, may suffer from underlying SEN, or they may be perfectly able but lack basic literacy skills, boundaries and self-esteem. Challenging behaviour can be understood as a defence mechanism or a cry for help. As a professional adult, do not allow conflict situations to escalate, but try to find out about and connect with the person behind the behaviour. Discover his or her hopes, dreams, interests and talents in order to achieve a productive working relationship.

Young people with behavioural, emotional and social difficulties (BESD) may struggle with RE because it often requires quiet attention to rather abstract ideas. However, RE can be of enormous importance in their journey towards adulthood in offering the opportunity to experience critical, balanced thinking and formulate their own considered opinions.

Of course, your boundaries must be firm and clear in order to create a space where interactive and collaborative learning is possible. You should already have a classroom code, expectations for how to treat each other, sanctions for breaking class rules and so on. This may involve seating plans, reward systems, expectations about how pupils enter the classroom or what happens if work is not completed. Establishing positive behaviour norms with young people with BESD is no different than with all young people, but it is of prime importance. The tips below may seem like extra work, but taking the time to plan and prepare for BESD pupils is never time wasted. This planning allows you to create an environment in which they can achieve and feel good about themselves. When they start to view themselves as 'good' rather than 'bad' pupils of RE, you can build on an increasingly positive and productive working relationship.

Top ten survival tips

1. Plan for poor behaviour; have your books and equipment ready so there are no breaks in a smooth-running lesson. Use pace to control behaviour; do not leave gaps that can be filled with chaos! Plan alternative activities, especially if the learning requires a certain amount of respectful attention. Plan to end the learning in a calm and orderly fashion. Line up a short video clip to watch while you collect books and check homework, or have a quiz planned for when the tables are tidy, etc.

2. Tidy as you go. The classroom is a working environment and should reflect order and productivity, not mess and confusion.

3. Know your pupils; chat to them as people, find out about them, take them seriously, become aware of friendship groups and particular talents you can utilise; use assessment data to identify strengths and weaknesses.

4. Differentiate – give out specific roles in group work, or differentiated tasks in individual work. Design learning activities that all pupils can access and engage in.

5. Don't 'dumb down'. Learning may be broken into manageable chunks, but the big questions should still be at the heart of what you do.

6. Focus on literacy. Design supportive tasks so pupils with poor literacy can still access the higher-order thinking skills.

7. Use assessment for learning; teach students how to be better learners, give them ownership over their own achievement.

8. Know your learning aims/learning outcomes; have a clear sense of what everyone needs to have achieved. Ensure all pupils have achieved your aims by the end of the lesson.

9. Choose your battles. Decide what you will and will not tolerate and stick to it. You may refuse to tolerate personal comments but let it slide if a pupil accidentally swears. Apply these expectations consistently to all pupils.

10. Model appropriate behaviour. Use humour to deflate conflict, retain control without abusing your authority, listen to pupils and treat everyone fairly.

Religious and Moral Education (RME) in non-denominational schools in Scotland is protected by legislation dating back to 1872 and continued in all relevant legislation and policy to the present day. RME is a mandatory subject for all pupils throughout their schooling. Also enshrined in legislation is the parents' right to withdraw children from RME. This withdrawal is rarely used, mostly as a consequence of the current nature and scope of RME being educational rather than confessional.

RME is designed to reflect the place of religions, beliefs and values in twenty-first century Scotland and to develop skills of criticality and discernment in young people. As a consequence, the vast majority of parents, educationalists and politicians regard RME as a fundamental, important and core element of Scottish education. This is reflected in the current curriculum guidance, Curriculum for Excellence.

Approximately 20 per cent of Scottish schools are faith based (denominational), predominantly Roman Catholic. These schools are fully state funded and follow the same curriculum, apart from in Religious Education, where there are separate guidelines based on the teachings of the Roman Catholic Church (Religious Education in Roman Catholic schools, RERC).

In all Scottish schools, denominational and non-denominational, the same key elements are core:

- recognition of the place of religion and belief in modern life
- learning about religions and non-religious traditions
- developing pupils' own perspectives on moral, philosophical and ethical issues
- developing the skills of criticality and discernment
- offering opportunities to put such knowledge and skills into practice in order to make a difference in the world.

Learning, teaching and assessment in RME

Personal search should permeate all RME, as pupils 'learn about' and 'learn from' religions and beliefs. This is core to encouraging the development of pupils' own beliefs and values.

Fundamental to a personal-search approach is the need for pupils to have the opportunity for personal reflection and exploration of the context for learning and the issues that arise.[16] An experiential and active learning approach to teaching and learning is suggested to achieve this by the 'Principles and Practice' document produced to assist teachers to plan effective learning and teaching.

Curriculum for Excellence overall advocates an interdisciplinary approach in order for pupils to see the connections between their learning and to allow them to apply previous knowledge to new contexts. While this is worthwhile, and RME is well placed to be delivered in an interdisciplinary context, care must be taken to ensure that progression and understanding in RME is achieved and tenuous links to topics are avoided.

Assessment in RME should take account of not only what pupils have learned about religions and beliefs, but what they have learned from this and to what extent they have been given an opportunity to develop and articulate their own beliefs and values.

---

[16] M Kincaid and R McVeigh, *Effective Teaching of Religious and Moral Education: Personal Search* (Learning and Teaching Scotland 2001).

Certification in RME

Since the 1980s RME has also evolved to offer a range of qualifications for pupils within and outside mandatory delivery. There are Scottish Qualification Authority (SQA) units and courses for pupils that typically cover three areas:

1 the study of a World Religion (i.e. Buddhism, Christianity, Hinduism, Islam, Judaism, Sikhism)

2 the study of ethics and morality in a range of contexts (i.e. Medical Ethics, War, Crime and Punishment, Sexuality, Gender, the Environment, Global Issues)

3 the study of philosophical issues relating to religion and other narratives (i.e. Science, Humanism, Marxism).

Pupils either study discrete units on these areas (typically on Morality) or can elect to study for courses covering all three areas in the senior phase of the secondary school. Given the increasingly philosophical nature of these materials, these subject qualifications are titled Religious, Moral and Philosophical Studies (RMPS).

For all relevant documents, see www.educationscotland.gov.uk/learningandteaching/ curriculumareas/rme

Entitlements to RE are established in law in the UK. This means that all students on roll, including all 14–19 year olds, must be provided with RE, apart from those withdrawn by their parents, or, for 18–19 year olds, by themselves. The public examination system covers the 14–19 curriculum, but not all students will take an exam in RS at 16. The statutory obligation to provide RE for all means decisions will have to be made about what mode of 14–19 RE is best for each student and each school. 16-year-olds in Scotland may take Standard Grade or Higher Grade Religious, Moral and Philosophical Studies (RMPS). Scottish candidates may also take an RMPS short course involving 40 hours of tuition. In Northern Ireland the Core Syllabus provides a basis from which schools can build an RE curriculum to suit their needs.

In England and Wales students may take a GCSE option, but for those who do not, non-examined RE should still be provided.

Weighing up taking external examinations in RS/RMPS	
Advantages	**Disadvantages**
• Working towards an examination gives RE/RS/RMPS status in the pupils' eyes. • Qualifications such as GCSEs, Standard Grades, Highers and A levels credit students' achievements and make them clear to the adult world and the world of work. • National syllabuses and external assessment can make RE more rigorous. • An RE department may strengthen its position in a school through examination success. • Examination success at 16+ may encourage young people to opt for Religious Studies at higher levels.	• National examinations may not fit well with local concerns or the local needs of your pupils. • GCSE and Standard Grade syllabuses do not cater for the full ability range and RE needs to offer opportunities to pupils of all abilities. • Working to an examination syllabus constrains what goes on in the RE classroom, leaving too little time for focus upon, for example, personal search. • The educational culture of over-assessment and functionalism is less likely to be challenged from within RE if the subject buys into examination culture.

Quality RE can be found on both sides of this continuing argument. If you decide to opt for the status and challenge of public examinations, the following questions may be useful when choosing a course:

• Does the course match the expertise of the teaching staff?

• Is the course recommended by colleagues teaching in similar schools?

• Does the course contain scope for teaching 'beyond the test'?

• Would you and your students find the course interesting in itself, quite apart from the qualification it offers?

• Does the mode of assessment suit your students' capabilities?

• If you are planning to offer a full course GCSE either as an option or for all students, will there be time allocated in the timetable? The required time is 140 hours of tuition.

If your school offers non-examined RE, which of these options would suit your students best?

- Follow the exam syllabus but do not take the exam.
- Follow the locally agreed syllabus.
- Design weekly RE lessons based on local interests and concerns.
- Design collapsed timetable 'RE days' three times a year, which could include a school trip.

In all of these cases, especially the replacement of weekly RE with RE days, you still need to ask whether provision builds a coherent and systematic understanding of religion, and how pupils will show progression in understanding and skills.

Examinations in RE

If you opt for a qualification in RS/RMPS, make sure you choose topics that you can really bring to life. You will spend a certain amount of time preparing your students to perform to the best of their ability in the exam, but plan to teach 'beyond the test'. The units at both GCSE/Standard level and A level/Higher level that make up the qualification can be of theological or social relevance beyond that of the qualification earned.

The 2015 revised GCSE criteria require study of two religions and offer opportunities to do textual study and religious, philosophical and ethical study. If you choose the *textual studies* element, you will be initiating your students into the methods and modes of analysis of the theologian, such as textual, source and historical analyses. Whether your students go on to take theology degrees or not, such a precise and demanding course will serve them in good stead for any analytical demands their futures may hold in various fields, such as economics and finance, the law, journalism or academia. Increasingly, universities recognise the value of an A level/Higher qualification in RS/RMPS even for students applying for science or maths subjects.

If you focus on the *religious, philosophical and ethical studies* element, you will be making important links for your students between the world's ancient stores of wisdom and today's most important ethical issues. These areas have been very popular in recent years because they allow students to explore classic philosophical and ethical conundrums, reflect on them for themselves and apply them to modern concerns. Again, teach 'beyond the test'; make sure the connections offered by the exam paper between ancient and modern are made meaningful in your classroom. Taught well, this subject discipline can be enormously valuable for students' political, social and ethical development.

Extended and Higher Projects

Some exam boards offer independent learning Higher Projects or Extended Projects at level 2 or level 3 equivalency. If you feel that a public examination will not stretch your students adequately, these additional projects may be for you. They offer a level of certification that may make it easier for you to request additional teaching hours. These projects provide a challenging learning experience for students, and the chance to test their skills of enquiry, research, analysis, extended writing and independent learning.

Non-examined RE

If you opt to deliver some RE without the structure of a public exam, ensure that you understand the difference between curriculum RE and enrichment.

Curriculum RE: This refers to the core RE provision, which is still a legal requirement for each pupil whether they take an exam or not, and should be equivalent to the hour a week of RE recommended for 14–16s (see p.18). Without the pressure of an exam, some teachers speak very positively of their experiences of non-examined curriculum RE. This would be suitable for students who find the process of preparing for a public exam demoralising and counterproductive. Even without a stressful exam, curriculum RE must still promote appropriate rigour and coherence. You must be able to monitor your students' progress and the RE they learn must still be meaningful and have educational value. However, in such a situation you are free to develop some innovative practice of your own that suits your students' particular needs, while still embodying good RE. Such innovations could include assessment methods, speakers, visitors, themes that are relevant to students and opportunities for debates, drama or creative expression of ideas.

Enrichment: This refers to the RE usually delivered post-16. In order to meet their RE and PSHE requirements, schools often develop an enrichment programme covering personal, ethical and social topics. Some enrichment programmes do not really meet the legal requirements for RE, as the RE content is not designed to be rigorous and it is not easy to say how students are making progress. This may cause problems given the priority given to the promotion of spiritual, moral, social and cultural development (SMSC) across the school in the September 2014 Ofsted framework. Therefore as the RE specialist you may well be asked to develop a more educationally meaningful enrichment programme post-16. This could be a great opportunity to embed a rigorous RE curriculum in a lively and creative series of RE days or afternoons. Students in the sixth form are finding their feet as young adults and love the chance to learn about and debate hot ethical and socio-political topics. Many teachers who develop such programmes for sixth formers report, after some initial persuasion, that students and teachers respond with energy and interest.

Note: RE is a requirement for those sixth form colleges that are constituted under school regulations. For sixth form colleges constituted under Further Education regulations, RE is not a requirement for all students, but must be provided for those students who wish to take it.

How does RE promote pupils' learning and development?

Essential knowledge in RE: what do we want pupils to know, understand and be able to do?

There is a debate in education generally about the place of core knowledge: is schooling mostly about mastering different disciplines, each of which describes an area of human experience through examples of the best that has been thought and discovered in human history? Or should education concentrate instead on building up skills, attitudes and competences that enable pupils to get ready to function in a fast-changing world? In RE, this debate is sometimes expressed sharply: are we aiming to communicate deep understanding of religions one by one and of the phenomenon of religion in some general sense? Or is RE about giving pupils critical tools and empathic capacities that will serve them well as they explore and construct meaning in their own lives? Those who want this debate to be polarised won't agree with the idea that we can have our cake and eat it.

Other sections of this book address how RE can enable spiritual development for the pupil (see pp.48–51). Here, however, we pause to consider whether there is an essential core of knowledge that the subject must convey to pupils. Take for granted that it will be taught with expert pedagogy and will be shown to relate to the lives of pupils, and then consider: What ought pupils to know about religion and religions? What can we teach in just an hour a week?

There have been successive attempts to encourage Britain's faith communities to agree to lists of religious content, and these are valuable: what the Jewish community wants all our children to know about Judaism is a good base point for designing a programme of study. How the many groups of British Christians see their religion should not be ignored as a starting point for understanding. But as well as this, RE teachers do well to use a set of concept clusters as lenses to examine each religion they study. These concept clusters can shape learning from any religion or worldview and make sense of our complex field of enquiry and knowledge. The concept clusters used in RE over the last 20 years are:

beliefs and teachings	sources of wisdom and authority	ways of living and ways of expressing meaning
questions of meaning, purpose and truth	questions of identity, diversity and belonging	questions of values and commitments

Now, immediately, the question of how many religions need to be studied arises. We take the view here that learning from one religion alone is not a complete British religious education. But learning from too many religions inevitably sacrifices depth of essential knowledge to breadth or superficial knowledge. So two religions are an essential platform for good RE, and more than two a desirable platform.

If pupils are to master essential knowledge about two or more religions, then they will need:

- a well-educated and religiously and culturally knowledgeable teacher
- an attitude of enthusiastic engagement with their studies
- programmes of learning designed to enable systematic understanding of religion and religions.

These needs actually match closely what is needed in RE for personal development. The essential knowledge that RE communicates goes hand in hand with a classroom approach that makes religions and worldviews a source of good learning for any – every – child. You *can* have your cake and eat it.

'Learning from religion': what does this mean?

One of English RE's most important – and internationally admired – concepts is 'learning from religion'. These pages explore this phrase's meanings and use for energising RE.

The original vision

In 1987, Michael Grimmitt introduced the concept of 'learning from religion' and established it as a key intention of the subject in his ground-breaking book *Religious Education and Human Development*.[17]

Grimmitt intended to address problems in RE that arose with the subject's founding by the 1944 Education Act. Since 1944, learning RE has been an entitlement for all, but by the 1980s two major questions remained unaddressed:

• Upon what basis could any child learn about religion(s), if not on the basis of religious nurture in a particular tradition, or religious commitment to a particular religious perspective?

• By what rationale was state funding of RE to be supported in a religiously plural and secularising society like the UK?

Today, it is clear that Grimmitt's framework has stood the test of time. Grimmitt wrote that RE must give pupils:

> . . . the opportunity to acquire skills which enable them to use their understanding of religion in the interpretation of their own personal experiences.[18]

His account of the purposes of RE centres on the learner, not on the religions. RE is to be in the service of the child or young person.

The meaning of 'learning from religion'

For Grimmitt, the concept of learning from religion is central to the processes of the kind of state-sponsored, plural RE that can be justified in the public arena. The concept is multidimensional, including these key ideas:

• **Anyone can learn from a religion.** The kinds of learning involved do not require acceptance of the convictions of a religion. An atheist or agnostic may learn from Christianity or Islam. A religious community can make a gift of human learning to the outsider without requiring that he or she become an insider.

• **Exploration of what it means to be human is at the heart of learning from religion.**

• **Learning from a religion not my own involves no sacrifice of integrity.** The processes of engagement, reflection and response draw upon empathic skills, use methods of dialogue, and challenge the learner to examine assumptions and presuppositions within a framework of honest disagreement and acceptance of diversity.

• **Learning from religion is an evaluative process.** The two kinds of evaluation that it requires are personal and impersonal, or critical. Where impersonal/critical evaluation draws upon many disciplines and uses analysis as its tool, personal evaluation responds to the challenges, influence and ideas of religion in ways that are profoundly connected to the identity of the learner (although not uncritically).

• **Learning from religion is a challenging process.** From the insight that diversity is a source of learning comes the sometimes uncomfortable possibility of discerning a challenge in the way of life or beliefs of those dissimilar to me. This challenge is not to coerce the non-Buddhist to become a Buddhist: it is to see the human condition from a perspective not my own. In this sense, learning from religion carries the possibility of personal transformation, but never the intention of conversion.

---

[17] Michael Grimmitt, *Religious Education and Human Development* (McCrimmons 1987).
[18] Ibid., p.216.

The use of 'learning from religion'

In 1994 the School Curriculum and Assessment Authority (SCAA) designed and published Model Syllabuses for RE to guide locally agreed syllabus conferences for English Local Education Authorities (LEAs). These models used two attainment targets, the second of which was 'Learning from Religion'. The inclusion of 'attainment target 2' in a large majority of syllabuses of RE for 20 years from 1994 gave wide influence to the concept of 'learning from religion'. However, because the concept was used to define an area of attainment rather than to describe the intentions of RE, this wide influence was sometimes at the expense of shallow understanding. Grimmitt's responses to the use (or was it appropriation?) of his concept are an interesting blend of negative and positive. In 2000, he wrote:

> . . . the effect of applying the [SCAA] model syllabuses to classroom RE, despite their adoption of learning about and learning from religion as the two attainment targets, has been to encourage teachers to fall back on a predominantly descriptive approach to the study of religions in which learning about religions is dominant. Where teachers attempt to encourage pupils to learn from religions, it falls far short of the pedagogical strategy which the original concept involved.[19]

Should 'learning from religion' still be an intention for RE?

What has happened to the original idea? Grimmitt writes that the original concept was that:

> . . . pupils should evaluate their understanding of self in religious terms . . . the evaluative process of learning from religion(s) should be fully integrated into how, within a secular educational context, pupils are learning about religion in the first place.[20]

This kind of learning from religion is not an attainment target but is instead a vision of purpose for the subject. This vision, frequently expressed in the context of attainment by government documentation, is often highly valued by teachers, who acknowledge very largely that learning from religion is the way of seeing RE that carries inspiration and possibilities of transformation for teachers and pupils.

---

[19] Michael Grimmitt (ed.), *Pedagogies of Religious Education: Case Studies in the Research and Development of Good Pedagogic Practice in RE* (McCrimmons 2000), p.15.

[20] Ibid.

Learning from religion in the 2013 Framework

The introduction to the Framework continues to use the concept of learning from religion:

In RE [pupils] learn about and from religions and worldviews in local, national and global contexts, to discover, explore and consider different answers to [questions about human identity, meaning and value]. They learn to weigh up the value of wisdom from different sources, to develop and express their insights in response, and to agree or disagree respectfully. Teaching therefore should equip pupils with systematic knowledge and understanding of a range of religions and worldviews, enabling them to develop their ideas, values and identities. It should develop in pupils an aptitude for dialogue so that they can participate positively in our society with its diverse religions and worldviews.[21]

The continuing focus on what learners get from their studies, which this concept provides, should encourage all teachers of RE to recognise that good RE always includes engagement, reflection, response and evaluation (personal and critical): the subject is not merely concerned with core knowledge, invaluable though this is.

Refreshing 'learning from religion'

Here are four ideas for the refreshing of 'learning from religion'. They reprise themes from Grimmitt's original analysis of 1987.

- RE teaching needs to promote engagement with religion and its challenges at every point. There is a continuing problem around RE teaching that is diminished to the mere collection of stuff about religions.
- The skills of engagement, reflection and response need to be tied in to the work teachers plan on core knowledge. This entwining can produce a holistic process of learning in RE, avoiding the dangers of dry factuality on the one hand and on the other of RE floating free of its roots in relation to living religious traditions.
- The evaluation of religious, spiritual and human questions that is the focus of the process of learning from religion needs the rigour of critical reflection and the development of skills in relation to the disciplines by which religion is studied. These disciplines include textual study, history, sociology, ethnography, psychology of religion, philosophy and theology.
- This critical evaluation needs also to be entwined with the development of skills of personal evaluation. This process can provide the learner with the space and skills to learn in personal ways that go far beyond the areas tested in examination Religious Studies. The ultimate questions of value, identity and truth face every human. RE enables learners to explore life in the light of the insights of living religions. Perhaps this is a main reason why a steady stream of visitors from many national education systems across the world continue to come looking admiringly at RE in the UK.

---

[21] *A Review of Religious Education in England* (REC 2013), p.14.

Skills for learning: what skills does RE develop in pupils?

Progress in RE involves the application of general educational skills and processes in handling subject knowledge. This, in turn, strengthens the skills and deepens understanding and knowledge. The following skills are important in RE and are reflected in many agreed syllabus programmes and approaches. You should plan to enable pupils to make progress with these skills as appropriate in each key stage, as you enable pupils to extend their subject knowledge.

RE teaching is intended to develop these skills:	Examples of progression from 5 to 16 – pupils will be increasingly able to:
Investigating – in RE, this includes abilities such as: • asking relevant questions • knowing how to use different types of sources as ways of gathering information • knowing what may constitute evidence for understanding religion(s).	• ask deep and complex questions about religion • use a widening range of sources to pursue answers • focus on selecting and understanding relevant sources to deal with religious and spiritual questions with increasing insight and sensitivity • evaluate a range of responses to the questions and issues they study.
Reflecting – in RE, this includes abilities such as: • reflecting on religious beliefs and practices and ultimate questions • reflecting upon feelings, relationships and experiences • thinking and speaking carefully about religious and spiritual topics.	• describe how action and atmosphere makes them feel • experience the use of silence and thoughtfulness in religion and in life • take increasing account of the meanings of experience and discern the depth of questions religion addresses • respond sensitively and with insight to religious and spiritual phenomena and their meanings.
Expressing – in RE, this includes abilities such as: • explaining concepts, rituals and practices • identifying and articulating matters of deep conviction and concern, and responding to religious issues through a variety of media.	• explain what words and actions might mean to believers • articulate their own reactions and ideas about religious questions and practices • clarify and analyse with growing confidence aspects of religion that they find valuable or interesting or negative • explain in words and other ways their own responses to matters of deep conviction.
Interpreting – in RE, this includes abilities such as: • drawing meaning from, for example, artefacts, works of art, poetry and symbols • interpreting religious language • suggesting meanings of religious texts.	• say what an object means, or explain a symbol • use figures of speech or metaphors to speak creatively about religious ideas • understand increasingly the diverse ways in which religious and spiritual experience can be interpreted • clarify and express the role of interpretation in religion and life.
Empathising – in RE, this includes abilities such as: • considering the thoughts, feelings, experiences, attitudes, beliefs and values of others • developing the power of imagination to identify feelings such as love, wonder, forgiveness and sorrow • seeing the world through the eyes of others; seeing issues from their point of view, deepening understanding of beliefs and practices.	• see with sensitivity how others respond to their actions, words or behaviour • connect their feelings, both positive and negative, with those of others, including those in religious stories and contexts • imagine with growing awareness how they would feel in a different situation from their own • identify thoughtfully with other people from a range of communities and stances for life.

RE teaching is intended to develop these skills:	Examples of progression from 5 to 16 – pupils will be increasingly able to:
Applying – in RE, this includes abilities such as: • using RE learning in new situations • making the association between religions and individual, community, national and international life • identifying key religious values and their connections with secular values.	• recognise religious materials and take note of their details and style • see links and simple connections between aspects of religions • make increasingly subtle and complex links between religious material and their own ideas • apply learning from one religious context to new contexts with growing awareness and clarity • synthesise their learning from different religious sources and their own ideas.
Discerning – in RE this includes abilities such as: • developing insight into personal experience and religion • exploring the positive and negative aspects of religious and secular beliefs and ways of life • relating learning to life • making thoughtful judgements about the personal value of religious beliefs and practices.	• experience the awe and wonder of the natural world and of human relations • be willing to look beyond the surface at underlying ideas and questions • weigh up the value religious believers find in their faith with insight, relating it to their own experience • discern with clarity, respect and thoughtfulness the impact (positive and negative) of religious and secular ways of living.
Analysing – in RE, this includes abilities such as: • distinguishing between opinion, belief and fact • distinguishing between the features of different religions • recognising similarity and distinctiveness between religious ways of life.	• see what kinds of reasons are given to explain religious aspects of life • join in discussion about issues arising from the study of religion • use reasons, facts, opinions, examples and experience to justify or question a view of a religious issue • analyse the religious views encountered with fairness, balance, empathy and critical rigour.
Synthesising – in RE, this includes abilities such as: • linking significant features of religion together in a coherent pattern • connecting different aspects of life into a meaningful whole • making links between religion and human experience, including the pupil's own experience.	• notice similarities between stories and practices from religions • use general words to describe a range of religious practice and teaching • make links between different aspects of one religion, or similar and contrasting aspects of two or more religions • explain clearly the relationships, similarities and differences between a range of religious arguments, ideas, views and teachings.
Evaluating – in RE, this includes abilities such as: • debating issues of religious significance with reference to experience, evidence and argument • weighing the respective claims of self- interest, consideration for others, religious teaching and individual conscience • drawing conclusions that are balanced, and related to evidence, dialogue and experience.	• talk about what makes people choose religious ways of life • describe how religious people demonstrate the importance of symbols, key figures, texts or stories • weigh up with fairness and balance the value they see in a range of religious practices • evaluate skilfully some religious responses to moral issues, and their own responses.

Developing attitudes: what attitudes can RE foster?

Attitudes such as respect for others and respect for the truth, care for all people and a determination to achieve should be promoted through all areas of school life. There are some attitudes, however, that are fundamental to RE. These attitudes enable learners to enter fully into the study of religions and beliefs and are in turn fostered and deepened by the study of RE.

Six key attitudes in RE	Examples of the ways RE can build and develop these attitudes
Self-awareness in RE includes pupils: • feeling confident about their own beliefs and identity and sharing them without fear of embarrassment or ridicule • developing a realistic and positive sense of their own religious, moral and spiritual ideas • recognising their own uniqueness as human beings and affirming their self-worth • becoming increasingly sensitive to the impact of their ideas and behaviour on other people.	**Pupils may be able to show self-awareness through:** • talking about their own way of life and different ways of life seen in some religions or worldviews • exploring what makes them special or unique in increasing depth • being able to value their own way of life as well as that of others • expressing and exploring their own sense of what matters most in human life, including reference to values and spirituality • using concepts such as identity, faith and culture to explain who they are and where they belong • analysing their own beliefs and values carefully and with reference to some religious alternatives • developing increasing self-confidence in tandem with empathic appreciation of others.
Respect for all in RE includes pupils: • developing skills of listening and a willingness to learn from others, even when others' views are different from their own • being ready to value difference and diversity for the common good • appreciating that some beliefs are not inclusive and considering the issues that this raises for individuals and society • recognising the rights of others to hold their own views • being prepared to recognise and acknowledge their own biases • appreciating that religious convictions are often deeply felt • being sensitive to the feelings and ideas of others.	**Pupils may be able to show respect for all through:** • talking about what is fair and unfair, just and unjust, for themselves and for others • the avoidance of ridicule • the development of tolerance and the move from tolerance to respect • applying ideas about fairness and respect from religious teachings to a range of situations • the widening and deepening of willingness to learn from others and respect the rights and views of all • considering questions about prejudice including issues around racism, ethnicity, sexuality, gender or religion and belief with reference to teachings about equality • analysing the causes and consequences of unfairness and suggesting how a more fair society can be built.
Open-mindedness and questioning in RE includes pupils: • being willing to learn and gain new understanding • engaging in argument or disagreeing reasonably and respectfully (without belittling or abusing others) about religious, moral and spiritual questions • being willing to go beyond surface impressions • having openness to points of view different from one's own	**Pupils may be able to show an attitude of open-mindedness through:** • beginning to use information and ideas from other people to answer big questions for themselves • talking about the reasons people give for their beliefs • describing how people react to the beliefs of others and beginning to see different sides to arguments about religious questions • showing that they can hold and justify opinions about religious and spiritual questions, referring to religious sources, arguments and experiences

• distinguishing between opinions, viewpoints and beliefs in connection with issues of conviction and faith.	• using evidence, reason and experience to express insights into religious or spiritual controversies • considering what makes some people narrow-minded or closed to new ideas, and what makes others open-minded • considering and explaining the differences between superstition, prejudice, opinion, belief, conviction and knowledge • applying the idea of open-mindedness critically to their own views as well as others' views.
Critical awareness in RE includes pupils: • having a willingness to examine ideas, questions and disputes about religious and spiritual questions • distinguishing between opinions, viewpoints and beliefs • being prepared to re-consider existing views • developing the ability to argue respectfully, reasonably and evidentially about religious and spiritual questions • being prepared to acknowledge bias and prejudice in oneself.	**Pupils may be able to show critical awareness through:** • beginning to notice that lots of RE questions have more than one answer that is interesting • talking about mysteries and puzzling things in RE • describing how people can argue about a belief in ways that weigh up both sides • showing that they can be self-critical about understanding beliefs and that they can criticise beliefs they don't agree with reasonably (i.e. without ridicule) • using evidence, reason and experience to make a critical commentary on beliefs they reject • explaining some strong and some weak arguments or reasons for holding a belief • interpreting the arguments and ideas of others in ways that are alert to accuracy, rationality, coherence and philosophical skills.
Commitment in RE includes pupils: • understanding the importance of commitment to a set of values by which to live one's life • showing willingness to develop a positive approach to life • developing the ability to learn, while living with certainty and uncertainty.	**Pupils may be able to show commitment through:** • talking about what matters most to them and what matters most to others • learning the meaning of the word 'commitment' and beginning to apply the idea for themselves • trying out and developing attitudes that value their own commitments and notice those of others • applying ideas about being committed to a religion, so that they see the impact of religious convictions for themselves • considering their own commitments carefully and facing the challenges of avoiding hypocrisy • reasoning and analysing examples of commitment that benefit humanity – and some that don't seem to.
Curiosity, appreciation and wonder in RE includes pupils: • developing their imagination and curiosity • recognising that knowledge is bounded by mystery • appreciating the sense of wonder at the world in which they live • developing their capacity to respond to questions of meaning and purpose.	**Pupils may be able to show curiosity, appreciation and wonder through:** • taking time to think and reflect in RE • engaging in and enjoying experiences that stimulate wonder • asking questions about the 'why' of religion, and suggesting answers that refer to religious teachings and their own ideas • being increasingly able to talk about mystery and about what is puzzling or profound in life • practising openness and thoughtful reflection on mysterious experiences and questions with increasing insight and discernment • analysing the differences between different religious viewpoints and accounting for these with discernment in their own terms.

Happiness and well-being: what has that got to do with RE?

Well-being can be interpreted in terms of healthy choices and lifestyles, and schools take their responsibility for supporting the well-being of children seriously. However, RE opens the possibility of exploring a deeper understanding of well-being, incorporating spiritual health, a fascination with the world and our place in it, and a resilience to the hardships that life often brings.

Many schools implement intervention strategies to hone pupils' skills and abilities in handling their emotions or developing resilience in the light of the pressures of life. Examples of such strategies include SEAL (Social and Emotional Aspects of Learning) and the Penn Resilience UK programme. Whilst there is a need for many pupils to develop these skills and abilities, such approaches often fail to place the idea of well-being within a wider philosophical and moral framework.

An example can be made by considering the idea of happiness, which most would agree has a significant place within human well-being. The term 'happiness' is used in a wide variety of ways. Five are given below.

Happiness as pleasure	Happiness as emotion	Happiness as life-satisfaction	Happiness as flourishing	Happiness as transcendence
It's all about having pleasant experiences (laughter, fun, excitement, chocolate, a great film) and avoiding bad ones.	It's about feelings and moods – feeling happy and content, enjoying life, although we know such feelings can come and go.	This is where you weigh up your life and think whether, in general, it is going OK in relation to your goals and ideals.	This is about developing your strengths and virtues, enabling you to handle the challenges of life. It involves your relationships with others.	This sense of happiness is tied in with a search for meanings and purposes, leading to a view that the significance of life extends beyond the material.

The intervention strategies mentioned above contribute to the first two strands of happiness. RE, on the other hand, explores all five, with particular emphasis on how religions and beliefs contribute to the ideas of happiness as life-satisfaction, flourishing and transcendence.[22]

HOW RE EXPLORES ALL FIVE STRANDS OF HAPPINESS

Happiness as pleasure	Happiness as emotion	Happiness as life-satisfaction	Happiness as flourishing	Happiness as transcendence
Within religions, celebrations can be an opportunity for fun and enjoyment. Pupils could compare some festivals, such as Holi or Diwali, Purim or Sukkot. These experiences are made more pleasant by the fact that they recall the defeat of unpleasant or bad events.	Religions deal with emotion and intellect. Stories of Noah, the Lost Son, Bhai Lalo and Malik Bhago, Prince Rama and Princess Sita – all of these concern moral behaviour but include strong emotional responses. Pupils explore the moral dimension of feelings by examining ideas of peace in Islam, gratitude in Judaism, or love in Christianity.	Life-satisfaction requires a sense of value; RE is a place to explore values and goals. Learning from religion includes a challenge: as pupils study Sikh service, Muslim charitable giving or Christian fasting, they have the opportunity to examine their own values and behaviour in the light of their learning.	RE helps pupils to explore what it means to be fully human, the idea of flourishing, whilst acknowledging the reality of pain, suffering and evil. RE explores the idea that human beings are flawed, and different explanations for this, as well as religious teachings that encourage believers to practise virtue.	RE has questions of meaning and purpose at its heart. It explores questions such as 'Who am I?' 'Who am I becoming?' 'How should we live?' 'What is the meaning of life?!' Comparing Hindu or Muslim goals for living with Buddhist and non-religious responses – all of these give pupils the opportunity to reflect on meaning and purpose for themselves.

---

[22] To explore this further, see S Pett, 'The Contribution of Religious Education to the Well-being of Pupils', *Research Papers in Education*, vol. 27, no. 4 (2012), pp.435–48.

Promoting 'British values': what role might RE play?

Since September 2014, school inspection in England has explored and judged the contribution schools make to actively promoting British values. RE can make a key educational contribution to pupils' explorations of British values, and excellent teaching of RE can enable pupils to learn to think for themselves about them.

Questions about whether social and moral values are best described as 'British values' or seen as more universal human values will continue to be debated (not least in the RE classroom!), but for the purposes of teaching RE, the subject offers opportunities to build an accurate knowledge-base about religions and beliefs in relation to values. This in turn supports children and young people so that they are able to move beyond attitudes of tolerance towards increasing respect, so that they can celebrate diversity.

Values education and moral development are a part of a school's holistic mission to contribute to the well-being of each pupil and of all people within our communities. The RE curriculum focuses learning in some of these areas, but pupils' moral development is a whole-school issue.

Mutual tolerance

Schools do not accept intolerant attitudes to members of the community: attitudes which reject other people on the basis of race, faith, gender, sexual orientation or age are rightly challenged. A baseline for a fair community is that each person's right to 'be themselves' is to be accepted by all. Tolerance may not be enough: RE can challenge children and young people to be increasingly respectful and to celebrate diversity, but tolerance is a starting point. It is much better than intolerance.

Respectful attitudes

In the RE curriculum, attention focuses on developing mutual respect between those of different faiths and beliefs, promoting an understanding of what a society gains from diversity. Pupils will learn about diversity in religions and worldviews, and will be challenged to respect other persons who see the world differently to themselves. Recognition and celebration of human diversity in many forms can flourish where pupils understand different faiths and beliefs, and are challenged to be broad-minded and open-hearted.

Democracy

In RE, pupils learn the significance of each person's ideas and experiences through methods of discussion. In debating the fundamental questions of life, pupils learn to respect a range of perspectives. This contributes to learning about democracy, examining the idea that we all share a responsibility to use our voice and influence for the well-being of others.

The rule of law

In RE, pupils examine different examples of codes for human life, including commandments, rules or precepts offered by different religious communities. They learn to appreciate how individuals choose between good and evil, right and wrong, and they learn to apply these ideas to their own communities. They learn that fairness requires that the law apply equally to all, irrespective – for example – of a person's status or wealth. They have the opportunity to examine the idea that the 'rule of law' focuses specifically on the relationship between citizens (or subjects) and the state, and how far this reflects or runs counter to wider moral codes and precepts.

Individual liberty

In RE, pupils consider questions about identity, belonging and diversity, learning what it means to live a life free from constraints. They study examples of pioneers of human freedom, including those from within different religions, so that they can examine tensions between the value of a stable society and the value of change for human development.

By its very nature, RE involves learning about others. RE teaching and learning should provide many opportunities to challenge stereotypical views and to appreciate difference positively. In RE we learn about and from people who have different beliefs and ideas with whom you may disagree or with whom you find yourself agreeing (perhaps to your surprise). In teaching about different religions and worldviews we aim to educate pupils to disagree or agree respectfully with the ideas they encounter.

Government guidance advises that 'every school is responsible for educating children and young people who will live and work in a country which is diverse in terms of cultures, religions or beliefs'. The government has set out its view of British values as including individual liberty, tolerance and mutual respect between those of different faiths and beliefs. The Ofsted *School Inspection Handbook* (September 2014) clearly notes the importance of respect in its description of pupils' spiritual and social development. However, this is most clearly shown in the handbook's description of pupils' cultural development. The cultural development of pupils is shown by their:

- *understanding and appreciation of the wide range of cultural influences that have shaped their own heritage and that of others*
- *understanding and appreciation of the range of different cultures within school and further afield as an essential element of their preparation for life in modern Britain …*
- *interest in exploring, improving understanding of and showing respect for different faiths and cultural diversity, and the extent to which they understand, accept, respect and celebrate diversity, as shown by their tolerance and attitudes towards different religious, ethnic and socio-economic groups in the local, national and global communities.[23]*

The 2013 *Review of Religious Education in England* says: '[RE] should develop in pupils an aptitude for dialogue so that they can participate positively in our society with its diverse religions and worldviews'.[24] Aim C (see page 3) also states that pupils should 'enquire into what enables different individuals and communities to live together respectfully for the wellbeing of all'. [25]

Promoting respect aims to contribute to reducing the corrosive effects of intolerance. It is too simplistic to assume that merely by teaching about the major world religions RE will automatically contribute to respect. It is even possible for weaker teaching to reinforce stereotypes. It is valuable to note that, for example, Christians, Jews and Muslims all give great significance to Jesus within their religious traditions, holding some aspects in common and diverging on other fundamental points. There is also, of course, great diversity within religions, where different interpretations can clash sharply. Pupils should learn about historical and current relationships between traditions, as well as ways in which religions have influenced each other's development.

RE is the ideal vehicle for building links with faith communities in the local area of the school. Pupils need opportunities to meet people of different faiths and cultures, to develop a respect for those who believe, think and practise differently, without feeling that their own identity or views are threatened. In fact, pupils can deepen and clarify their sense of identity through their encounter with the 'other'. It is important to set ground rules for discussion when religious differences are explored, in order to create a safe and positive environment. This is particularly relevant where there may be media misrepresentations and commonly held negative stereotypes, e.g. Islamophobic ideas, or unfair negativity to any religion.

It is also important to be clear that, whilst we value tolerance, there are clearly some sentiments and behaviours that we do not tolerate. Ofsted describes a spiritually developed person as one who is ready to challenge 'all that would constrain the human spirit, for example, poverty of aspiration, lack of self-confidence and belief, moral neutrality or indifference, force, fanaticism, aggression, greed, injustice, narrowness of vision, self-interest, sexism, racism and other forms of discrimination'.[26]

---

[23] *School Inspection Handbook* (Ofsted September 2014), para. 134.
[24] *A Review of Religious Education in England* (REC 2013), p.14.
[25] Ibid., p.15.
[26] *Promoting and Evaluating Pupils' Spiritual, Moral, Social and Cultural Development* (Ofsted 2004), p.13.

Promoting respect in RE includes pupils:

- developing skills of listening and a willingness to learn from others, even when others' views are different from their own
- being ready to value difference and diversity for the common good
- appreciating that some beliefs are not inclusive and considering the issues that this raises for individuals and society
- being prepared to recognise and acknowledge their own bias.

Ideas for the teacher

- Plan tasks that make pupils think more deeply about respect. For example, explore prejudice and its consequences and respect and its consequences when looking at relevant units or investigations.
- Make regular and meaningful links between what pupils are learning about in RE and the implication of these for their own values and society generally today: for example, learning about and applying the teachings of religious traditions and leaders to real-life situations in pupils' own experience.
- Ensure RE classrooms provide both safe and challenging spaces in which pupils' religions and beliefs are respected, whilst at the same time offering opportunity for rigorous critical enquiry.
- Be aware of your own assumptions and beliefs, and the fact that no one is 'neutral' or entirely objective when it comes to matters of beliefs and values.
- Adults set personal examples of integrity by being truthful, admitting ignorance or uncertainty when necessary.

Ideas for the classroom

- Allow pupils to encounter people who hold different religious and non-religious beliefs. There are many ways to do this, such as going on visits and inviting visitors into the classroom.
- For younger pupils, the use of persona dolls can help to introduce a different religion in a way that engages the interest of pupils.
- Welcome families and friends from different communities to the school when you are learning about religious festivals.
- Enable pupils to interview faith community representatives face to face or using tools such as Skype or Twitter, and use their research with other classes.
- Develop links, such as school twinning, and pupil encounter that focuses on respect and community issues.
- When studying a particular religion, spend time looking at the statistics about numbers of people from the religious community in your area or neighbouring area. Many people believe certain communities represent a higher percentage of the population than they do. Create a quiz or set up an investigation using census statistics to support this work.
- Look carefully at shared beliefs of some religions and where these beliefs differ. For example, consider the similarities and differences between the narratives of Noah/Nuh, Abraham/Ibrahim, Isaac and Ishmael/Ismail in Islam and Judaism. Consider differences of understanding on the status of Jesus/Isa, e.g. as Messiah or Christ for Christians, as a Jewish teacher for Jewish people, as a prophet of Islam.
- Find out about examples of interfaith work in your area or nearby, e.g. The Inter Faith Network. Have different faiths worked on shared social justice projects? Are there shared celebrations such as interfaith weeks?
- Consider teachings from different religions about dealing with difference, e.g. responses of respect, tolerance, mutual learning and recognition of each other's spirituality rather than mere argument or even conflict.
- Weigh up examples of how people have dealt well with difference or conflict. Give pupils some scenarios to think about in which people choose conflict or acceptance, hostility or tolerance.

Literacy: how can good literacy promote learning in RE?

Reading, writing, speaking and listening, the four strands of literacy, can be supported and developed through good RE. However, it is essential that RE outcomes and objectives remain the first thing for teachers to consider when planning RE. The links between literacy and RE are much wider than the specific objectives in the English National Curriculum or programme of study in England, Wales or Northern Ireland, or statements in the Curriculum for Excellence in Scotland. They link to reading and writing of different texts, interpreting meaning, discussion, debate, expression of opinion and much more.

Common ground

As we educate our pupils to be literate we want them to be able to communicate, interpret and respond. This supports pupils in thinking logically and using their imagination and creativity. These skills are fundamental to self-expression and to the understanding of other people.

Religious literacy includes knowing about, responding to and communicating beliefs, values and insights. This involves understanding, analysing and interpreting the symbols, beliefs, practices and structures of different religions and worldviews, and responding critically and empathetically to the challenges of belief and commitment in the world. Thus literacy and RE share common ground. Both, in their different ways, are about 'meaning making'.

Literacy skills

Reading
In RE we support pupils to:
- read with understanding
- identify the type of writing
- identify and understand technical language
- locate and use information
- interpret symbolic language
- follow the *process* of an argument, summarise, synthesise and adapt from reading (older pupils).

Writing
In RE we support pupils to:
- write different types of text, both fiction and non-fiction
- express their own ideas, arguments and evaluations
- creatively express ideas and thoughts through poetry, fiction and drama writing
- explain different points of view
- use and spell technical language accurately.

Speaking and listening
In RE we support pupils to:
- explore and share ideas
- refine thinking to share ideas more clearly
- express their ideas coherently and accurately
- challenge their thinking and the thinking of others
- hypothesise
- agree consensus or agree to differ
- listen to others and take account of their point of view
- understand others, taking into account their cultural background and religious belief or worldview
- share, interpret and understand religious belief and ideas using role play and drama.

A good RE subject leader will:
- make links to what is being taught in the English curriculum – where appropriate – when forming a long-term plan for RE
- identify literacy and English-based activities and tasks that promote effective RE learning, giving opportunities to learn through speaking and listening, reading and writing
- ensure that RE teaching and learning activities reinforce learning in English and literacy at appropriate times, for example, providing a context for developing an argument
- ensure RE work is marked first in relation to the RE learning outcomes and then, if appropriate, mark with reference to literacy or English outcomes
- monitor the stretch and challenge of literacy-based work in RE, ensuring that it at least matches expectations within English or literacy lessons

- identify and fulfil training needs with regard to RE and literacy
- share RE's contribution to improving literacy with senior leaders.

Developing literacy in RE

The following questions act as 'prompts' for teachers to consider how you can improve specific literacy skills in and through RE and at the same time improve the quality of pupils' oral and written expression in RE.

Reading and writing: key questions

- How do the range and quality of reading and writing opportunities help pupils develop the skills they need to enhance their learning in RE? How do we know?
- What opportunities do pupils have to read and write with confidence, fluency and understanding?
- How do we encourage them to develop an interest in words and their meanings and a growing vocabulary (generally and in relation to RE)? How do we help them to understand subject-specific words better?
- Do we give pupils opportunity to consider different types of text?
- Do we ask them to compare and contrast different accounts of the same incident? Do they consider expression and bias?
- Do pupils respond in different ways, e.g. comprehension, précis, story writing, writing for different audiences, poetry, essay, project or report writing? Do they get opportunities to draft and redraft their RE work?
- Do we use writing frameworks and sentence starters to support writing?
- How does what pupils do in RE compare with the range (and level of support/challenge) offered in and through other subject areas?

Speaking and listening: key questions

- How do the range and quality of speaking and listening opportunities help pupils develop the skills they need to enhance their learning in RE? How do we know?
- How often do pupils speak about an issue in different groupings (pairs, threes, fours, as a class)? How confidently do they do that? How do we provide discussion frameworks to improve their confidence?
- How well do individuals present information and ideas about religious and moral issues orally? How can we improve the range of opportunities to do so and the quality of their expression of ideas?
- Do our pupils listen carefully and respectfully to others? Do they understand what is being said and use it to further discussion? Can pupils put forward 'both sides of an argument'? Can they give valid reasons for their opinions in an articulate way?

Three examples of RE promoting literacy

Ask pupils to create a set of instructions for a minister (or leader in another Christian tradition): 'How to baptise a baby.' This can be enacted with a doll from the children's instructions. Other 'baby welcoming ceremonies' could be used for different groups.

Ask pupils to prepare for a debate on whether it is right to eat meat. They should present a range of views clearly and in a balanced way, including a Hindu understanding of the concept of ahimsa, non-harming, and some Christian interpretations of the concept of dominion. Evaluate orally and in writing, expressing reasoned responses and offering their own insights.

After studying Buddhist and Christian beliefs about life after death, encourage careful reading of texts for understanding and interpretive skills by tangling up two texts. For example, take Dhammapada 147–151 and 2 Corinthians 4:16–5:10 and mix them up. Ask pupils to disentangle the beliefs expressed in the texts, noting, explaining and accounting for similarities and differences.

Active learning in RE: what are the benefits?

There are many reasons why teaching should be active in the classroom:

- it will be more interesting for pupils and teachers
- it can help pupils to process the ideas rather than simply regurgitate them
- it will open up the possibility of new thinking and creativity, getting pupils to stretch their thinking beyond their own experience
- it can suit the needs of a range of different personalities, characters, abilities and ages in the classroom.

There is no substitute for thoughtful planning and the use of rich and stimulating content, of course, but active learning can contribute to good learning. There is some evidence to suggest that the major impact of many classroom interventions is down to teacher enthusiasm, rather than the benefits of the intervention itself. Your energy and enthusiasm in the classroom are vital, and developing active learning with your pupils can both reveal and support this.

Active learning has long been at the centre of the experience of the child in Early Years settings, where investigating and exploring, engaging with real-world experiences, and planned and spontaneous play support the focused teaching and learning that goes on. However, active learning strategies are not only for the very young, but can support successful learning for pupils and adults.

Some theories

Some writers argue that enquiry-based learning is the only way that people learn.[27] Others argue that such approaches overload the working memory and do not result in pupils laying down information in their long-term memory.[28] A middle way might be to say that if pupils have some knowledge, applying it to an open-ended problem can make them use it in ways that require and deepen understanding. Some have characterised this as the difference between surface learning (which takes time to develop) and deep learning (where the links between ideas make sense and begin to add to a coherent picture). Both phases are important, but pupils need to start with surface learning each time they begin a new area of study, so that gradually they are able to make links between different areas.[29] Surface learning need not be dull learning, of course! It is important to enable pupils to learn lots of stuff in active ways.

The examples of active learning strategies mentioned in the following sections can be found in *More Than 101 Great Ideas*, edited by Rosemary Rivett (RE Today 2013).

Films and resources are available here: www.natre.org.uk/primary/good-learning-in-re-films.

---

[27] E.g. Joanna Swann, *Learning, Teaching and Education Research in the 21st Century* (Continuum 2012).

[28] E.g. Paul A Kirschner et al., 'Why Minimal Guidance During Instruction Does Not Work: An Analysis of the Failure of Constructivist, Discovery, Problem-Based, Experiential, and Inquiry-Based Teaching', *Educational Psychologist*, vol. 41, no. 2 (2006), pp.75–86.

[29] See Daniel Willingham, *Why Don't Students Like School?* (Jossey-Bass 2009).

Some practical suggestions

Acting

The idea of pupils acting can make teachers fearful, but the types of activity you might use are strategies that provide pupils with opportunities to express their ideas in an active and expressive way, not by creating complicated performances. When learning is active, it is remembered, enjoyed and understood better. As the learners become more involved in the process of their own learning they move to draw conclusions from their own thinking and reflection.

Strategies such as freeze-framing, body sculpture, hotseating or creating a virtual news report allow pupils to process the knowledge they have gained about a religious story, leader or belief and apply this learning.

See www.youtube.com/watch?v=cEmocjWgx5E for an active telling of the story of Bilal in Islam with 5–6 year olds.

Creating

Religions are of themselves creative things. Every religion has phases of dynamic and stimulating creativity. In many religions beautiful buildings are created as a way of offering worship; art is created to honour God; sacred texts include various forms of writing – songs, poetry, letters and narrative; some religions use song, music and dance as part of their celebration and worship. Young children are naturally creative as they explore and learn, whether with construction toys or creating games and dens in outside space.

Creative RE allows pupils to generate something original, or involves thinking or behaving imaginatively, or tackles questions and ideas that are new to them.

Examples of creative strategies include picture extending, writing poetry or making music.

See www.youtube.com/watch?v=2besi23pDnY to see a creative way of exploring art in Islam.

Enquiring

Enquiring RE begins with young children: their first skills as enquirers come from exercising curiosity and pursuing the will to discover. This leads to increasingly sophisticated research, in which pupils investigate for themselves, set their own agendas for learning and become researchers in simple ways.

By setting enquiry tasks or providing supported opportunities for pupils to enquire into their own RE-relevant questions, pupils become more engaged with the subject. Learning is perceived as being more relevant to their own needs, thus they are enthusiastic and ready to learn.

Example of enquiry strategies include P4C (Philosophy for Children), asking and analysing questions, enquiring into a picture or artefact, and mystery strategies.

See www.youtube.com/watch?v=Jt-w4CrRzOc for a short film on enquiring into worship in Christianity with 7–9 year olds.

Reflecting

Reflection is the opportunity to step back and consider the ideas, understandings and questions that are being presented in RE. The skills of reflection include noticing, listening and attentiveness. Reflective RE can involve both silence and debate.

In good reflective RE pupils engage with the stimulus for learning but also engage with religious and spiritual materials for themselves and respond with their own developing insights.

Examples of reflection strategies include conscience or reflection alley, stilling and guided story.

See www.youtube.com/watch?v=t5dIBTz-gao for a 'reflection alley' in action with 9–11 year olds exploring the story of the centurion in Luke's Gospel.

Talking

Talking is essential to the learning process in any subject. In RE, good teaching can model, structure and guide the way pupils talk about religion and worldviews, so that they learn a lot from one another and the material they are discussing. Talk also clarifies things for the person doing the talking.

Pupils often say that they especially value RE for the range of discussion and argument it provokes. Talking and listening purposefully in RE supports pupils in remembering and processing the ideas and concepts with which they are engaging.

Discussion and debate in RE – where pupils critically engage with ideas and beliefs with which they sometimes disagree – is an opportunity to develop skills that will support them in adult life and employment.

Examples of talking strategies include debating, 'just a minute' and mystery bag.

Thinking

Pupils make progress in RE if they can compare different examples, identify and explain similarities and differences, rank, sort and order examples. Their RE tasks need to include making balanced judgements, noticing implications and possibilities, speculating or arguing effectively and analysing and synthesising information. The RE classroom should be a place that encourages and supports pupils to think.

RE planning should include teaching and learning where pupils carefully observe, discern the meaning of texts, research, clarify ideas and think deeply about concepts and issues.

Examples of thinking strategies include odd one out, mind mapping, feelings graph and fact or opinion.

See www.youtube.com/watch?v=YgrdpHdsYKc for a thinking skills lesson on sanctity of life.

Writing

Sometimes teachers note that pupils show good skills in discussion, but do not capture their best ideas in writing. In RE, writing tasks need to be imaginative, structured and set at a level that reflects what pupils are capable of in relation to the English curriculum for their age. Writing needs to be purposeful and, where possible, have a clear audience, real or imagined. Writing for our very youngest pupils needs an interesting stimulus and accessible vocabulary. Older children need writing tasks that develop ideas and concepts and promote reflection, thinking and evaluation.

Examples of writing strategies include disentangling two texts, 'on the one hand … on the other hand' and silent conversations.

What we now call spiritual, moral, social and cultural development (SMSC) has always been part of education. The notion of developing not just academic and practical skills in the emerging generation but also self-knowledge, moral courage, a capacity for imaginative sympathy for others and so on has long been a desired outcome of education. Over the decades this has been incorporated in a number of policies such as Every Child Matters and Community Cohesion, terms that refer to the sort of person an education system hopes to create.

SMSC has been the way this wider development of the whole person has been expressed in education policy since the 1944 Education Act. The 2013 National Curriculum articulates the purpose of education like this:

> *Every state-funded school must offer a curriculum which is balanced and broadly based[30] and which:*
>
> * *promotes the spiritual, moral, cultural, mental and physical development of pupils at the school and of society, and*
> * *prepares pupils at the school for the opportunities, responsibilities and experiences of later life.[31]*

The Ofsted school inspection handbook makes it clear that inspectors must consider the spiritual, moral, social and cultural development of pupils when making judgements about the overall effectiveness of a school. Schools will be considered to have serious weaknesses if 'there are important weaknesses in the provision for pupils' spiritual, moral, social and cultural development'.[32]

In terms of RE, there are two specific points to note. Firstly, although RE does make an enormous contribution to SMSC development, this is a *whole-school* responsibility. RE lessons should support the school's overall ethos. They may offer more in the way of spiritual or moral education than other subjects and RE teachers may enjoy working on SMSC-related projects with other colleagues, but every subject and every teacher has a duty to promote pupils' SMSC development. Secondly, the increased priority of SMSC from September 2014 should not mean more work for the average RE teacher. RE lesson content, skills and resources are already rich in SMSC. You may conduct a quick audit to gain an overview of your SMSC provision, or when creating a new display you may decide to give it an SMSC focus, but you should not have to produce more than the high-quality RE you already produce.

Below are tips and ideas for each category of SMSC. Use them as a checklist for an audit, to start a discussion in a staff meeting, or when selling a new RE project to your senior leaders. Many activities in your classroom will meet more than one of these criteria. You should not be reinventing the wheel, but realising how much SMSC you already provide.

Activities for spiritual development in RE

The 'spiritual' should not be confused with 'religious'. Spiritual development refers to the aspects of the child's spirit that are enhanced by school life and learning, and may describe the 'spirit' of determination, sharing or open-mindedness. Spiritual development describes the ideal spirit of the school. RE can support this by promoting:

* **Self-awareness:** offering opportunities for pupils to reflect on their own views and how they have been formed, as well as the views of others
* **Curiosity:** encouraging pupils' capacity for critical questioning, such as by keeping big questions in a 'question box' or as part of a wall display, and allowing time and space where these questions can be addressed to show that they are important

---

[30] See Section 78 of the 2002 Education Act, which applies to all maintained schools. Academies are also required to offer a broad and balanced curriculum in accordance with Section 1 of the 2010 Academies Act.

[31] *Statutory Guidance, National Curriculum in England: Framework for Key Stages 1 to 4* (DfE 2014 update), Section 2.1.

[32] *School Inspection Handbook* (Ofsted September 2014), para. 103.

- **Collaboration:** utilising lesson techniques that engender group collaboration and communication, such as community of enquiry/P4C, circle time, debates, Socratic circles or group investigations
- **Reflection:** providing a space to reflect on pupils' own values and views, as well as those of others, and to consider the impact of these values
- **Resilience:** promoting a spirit of open enquiry into emotive or complicated questions in order to learn how to cope with difficult ideas when they arise in the future
- **Response:** exploring ways in which pupils can express their responses to demanding or controversial issues
- **Values:** promoting an ethos of fairness and mutual respect in the classroom and compassion and generosity in pupils through exploring inspiring examples of these qualities in others
- **Appreciation:** encouraging pupils' ability to respond with wonder and excitement by exploring some of the marvels and mysteries of the natural world, of human ingenuity, and examples of the capacity of humans to love, create, organise and overcome adversity.

Activities for moral development in RE

Moral development is about exploring and developing pupils' own moral outlook and understanding of right and wrong. It is also about learning to navigate the fact of moral diversity in the world. RE is extremely well suited to exploring social and personal morality in significant ways.

 Valuing others: in exploring the views of others, young people are well prepared in RE to appreciate the uniqueness of all humans and their moral value, and to act in the world and towards others accordingly.
In the classroom: offer activities that enable teamwork and trust and require empathy. Welcome speakers or visit places of worship to learn from people of different backgrounds; explore case studies centring on forgiveness, generosity and other beneficial social moral values; use puppets, toys or persona dolls with younger children to develop their sense of moral connection with others.

 Moral character development: RE offers a safe space where pupils can learn from their mistakes, appreciate ideas of right and wrong, continue to strive after setbacks, take the initiative, act responsibly and demonstrate resilience. RE should present pupils with the challenge of responding in real and concrete ways to some of the moral questions they face.
In the classroom: encourage your pupils to take part in whole-school endeavours to enlarge their characters. Involve them in establishing appropriate moral codes for classroom, school and the wider community. Suggest participation on the school council or the school play, in sport, music and debates, to contribute to charity events or take part in mentoring or 'buddy' schemes.

Moral diversity: activities in RE lessons should help pupils feel confident when taking part in debates about moral issues. Debates and discussions should prepare pupils for the fact that there will always be disagreement on matters of morality and their right of expression is balanced by a responsibility to listen to the views of others.

In the classroom: choose age-appropriate topics that allow exploration of different moral outlooks, such as religious texts about right and wrong, codes for living, treatment of animals and the environment, gender roles in religion, religious views of homosexuality, and so on.

Activities for social development in RE

Social development refers to the ways young people are shaped in schools with an eye on the sort of society we wish to create in the future. Developing children and young people socially means giving them the opportunities to explore and understand social situations and contexts they may encounter in school or outside. In the RE classroom, such social situations may include exploring:

- **Shared values:** opportunities to consider values that are or should be part of society, such as those associated with right and wrong, treatment of others or diversity

- **Idealised concepts:** topics that require reflection on the abstract concepts our society is built on, such as justice, fairness, honesty and truth, and specific examples of how they affect our common life, such as in relation to how people treat each other in the classroom and school, issues of poverty and wealth, crime and punishment

- **Moral sources:** a chance to reflect on *where* ideas about how we should behave come from, whether religious or non-religious texts, teachings or traditions, in order to more fully understand social and behavioural norms

- **Influences:** opportunities to explore and reflect on the great influence on individuals of family, friends, the media and wider society, in order to understand how our behaviour is affected for good or ill

- **Social insight:** a chance to acquire insight into significant social and political issues that affect individuals, groups and the nation, such as how churches and gurdwaras may contribute practically to needs in their local communities, or how some religious and non-religious charities fight to change government policies where they are unjust

- **Role models:** teachers should model the sort of behaviour we expect of our children and young people, and RE should explore role models from the famous such as Desmond Tutu to local examples in the school and its community

- **Experiential learning:** pupils should have opportunities to embody for themselves expected behavioural and social norms, whether through class discussions, group work and ongoing behaviour expectations, or through special events such as school visits or drama workshops.

Activities for cultural development in RE

There are two meanings associated with 'cultural' development, and RE embodies both of them. Firstly, the term refers to the pupils' own home culture and background, whether religious or not, and secondly, the term describes our national culture. Schooling should prepare all young people to participate in Britain's wider cultural life, whatever their own background. Cultural development could be evident in RE in two major ways:

(1) Own culture: RE is the perfect subject in which to explore Britain's rich diversity of religious, ethnic and geographical cultures. Although all children share Britain's common life, cultural diversity is part of that life, and no child should feel their cultural background is a barrier to participation. Some common RE activities that promote children's understanding of communities and cultural groups, including their own, could include:

In the classroom: explore food, festivals, music, art, architecture and other forms of religious and cultural expression. Where possible, visit areas with a strong cultural flavour to observe shops, cafés, people and houses. Some parents may be willing to come and talk about their home culture, or send personal artefacts such as books, photos or clothes to school with their children. Students who belong to a particular cultural group should be encouraged to share their experiences in class discussion, give a talk or even an assembly.

(2) Wider culture: schooling is a preparation for adult life in terms of behaviour and expectations as well as in achieving qualifications. This wider cultural education prepares children for adulthood.

In the classroom: cultural education is found whenever children make sense of the world around them and explore why we act the way we do. Provide opportunities for participation in classroom and whole-school events, including art, music, drama, sport, activism and serving others; explore what it is like to encounter difficulties in learning and relationships and be open about the sorts of behaviours that are expected.

In England, Scotland and Northern Ireland, children are in the Foundation Stage until they finish the year in which they have their fifth birthday. In Wales, Foundation Phase describes the period from age 3 to age 7, combining the Early Years (3–5) and 5–7 year olds.

Children aged 4 or 5 who are on the school roll in the Reception class should be taught RE according to the appropriate syllabus (for example, the locally agreed syllabus). This does not apply to children who are withdrawn according to the wishes of their parents. In Scotland, children are taught according to the experiences and outcomes of the Early stage of RME in the Curriculum for Excellence (see pp.24–25).

It is important that teachers note that the requirement for RE differs from that of other subjects in the curriculum. RE becomes compulsory in the Reception class whereas National Curriculum subjects start in Year 1.

Legal requirements

Foundation Stage: Nursery (age 3–4)

- RE is non-statutory
- practitioners may incorporate RE material into children's activities if they choose
- Early Learning Goals (Desirable Outcomes in Wales) outline what children should achieve by the end of Reception. In Scotland, children work towards the experiences and outcomes in the Early stage of RME in the Curriculum for Excellence.

Foundation Stage: Reception (age 4–5)

- RE is a compulsory part of the basic curriculum for all Reception pupils
- RE should be taught according to the locally agreed syllabus for RE, diocesan guidelines or syllabus selected or written by your academy or free school
- Early Learning Goals (Desirable Outcomes in Wales) outline what pupils should achieve by the end of Reception. In Scotland, children work towards the experiences and outcomes in the Early stage of RME in the Curriculum for Excellence.

Year 1 onwards

- RE is compulsory for all pupils, except those withdrawn by their parents
- RE should be taught according to the locally agreed syllabus for RE, diocesan guidelines or syllabus selected or written by your academy or free school. In Scotland, children work towards the experiences and outcomes in the Early stage of RME in the Curriculum for Excellence.

What do pupils get out of RE in this age group?

RE sits very firmly within the areas of personal, social and emotional development and understanding the world. This framework enables children to develop a positive sense of themselves, and others, and learn how to form positive and respectful relationships. They will do this through a balance of guided, planned teaching and pursuing their own learning within an enabling environment. They will begin to understand and value the differences between individuals and groups within their own immediate community. Children will have opportunity to develop their emerging moral and cultural awareness.

Key areas of learning

Children should be provided with opportunities in RE to:

- listen to and talk about appropriate stories that engage them
- directly experience religion – engage with artefacts, visit places of worship (with a focus on experiences and symbols); listen and respond to visitors from faith communities
- get to know and use religious words accurately, e.g. God, Bible, mosque, prayer
- use all five senses – smell (e.g. incense), taste (e.g. special foods), see and touch (e.g. religious artefacts), hear (e.g. chants/hymns/prayers/bells)

- make and do – make festive food, role-play, dress up, dance
- have times of quiet and stillness
- share their own beliefs, ideas and values
- talk about their ideas and experiences and develop empathy for others
- use their imagination and curiosity to develop their appreciation and wonder of the world in which they live
- ask questions that are philosophically challenging and have them taken seriously
- begin to use ICT to explore religious beliefs as practised in the local and wider community.

Early Learning Goals

In England the Early Learning Goals that most closely relate to Religious Education are:

Communication and language

- **Listening and attention:** how children listen, including listening to stories, songs and poems from a range of different communities and religions; responding to what they hear with relevant comments, questions or actions; giving attention to what others say and respond appropriately, while engaged in another activity
- **Understanding:** how children answer 'how' and 'why' questions about their experiences and in response to stories, experiences or events from different sources
- **Speaking:** how children express themselves effectively, talking about how they and others show feelings, developing their own narratives and explanations by connecting ideas or events.

Personal, social and emotional development

- **Managing feelings and behaviour:** how children view themselves and others, talking about a positive sense of themselves and others; developing positive relationships and respect; getting on with others by understanding and handling their own feelings as well as recognising the feelings of others; talking about their own and others' behaviour and its consequences; recognising that some behaviour is unacceptable; working as part of a group or class, understanding and following the rules; developing confidence and keeping going in the face of difficulties in learning
- **Self-confidence and self-awareness:** how children show confidence, trying new activities, speaking in a familiar group, talking about their ideas and choosing appropriate resources
- **Making relationships:** how children play co-operatively, taking account of one another's ideas; showing sensitivity to others' needs and feelings; forming positive relationships with adults and other children.

Understanding of the world

- **People and communities:** talking about past and present events in their own lives and in the lives of family members; knowing that other children don't always enjoy the same things and being sensitive to this; knowing about similarities and differences between themselves and others, and among families, communities and traditions.

Expressive arts and design

- **Being imaginative:** using their imagination in art, music, dance, imaginative play, role play and stories to represent their own ideas, thoughts and feelings using a range of media; respond in a variety of ways to experiences through their senses.

Visits and visitors in RE: how can we make the most of these opportunities?

Visits are a useful resource and add another dimension to RE by providing pupils with the opportunity of experiencing religion as a living, vibrant community. Visits can be used as a stimulus to start a piece of work or to reinforce learning undertaken in the classroom.

Encounter and dialogue with people of different religions and beliefs is a key way of encouraging and developing respect. It is also a key way of building understanding of the role religion and beliefs play in the lives of individuals and communities. Both are important aims of RE.

Guidance for teachers planning a pupil visit to a place of worship

There are many benefits to be derived from visiting places of worship, but in practical terms you will need to think through the points listed below.

Before you go:

- **Make initial contact with the faith community** to find out if you can visit and when is the best time (both for you and the faith community).

- **Try to visit the faith community yourself** to explore learning opportunities and to discuss your needs with the person who will be involved in the visit. Share with him or her what you hope pupils will get out of the visit. Clearly planned aims help to fit the visit into a scheme of work. A general 'look around' is the least likely activity to be successful. If possible, try to arrange for the pupils to meet some believers other than leaders. Talk about how long you will stay. As a rule of thumb, under an hour is usually too short to make the most of the learning opportunity.

- **Get parental permission** – schools should send a letter home with each pupil to make clear that this is an educational visit and that pupils will observe, not participate in, worship. Invite parents and other adults to help out on the visit.

- **Prepare pupils.** This is likely to be a completely new situation for them. Provide guidance about appropriate attitudes and any dress requirements such as removing shoes, covering heads.

- **Prepare the learning** – encourage pupils to ask and respond to questions during the visit; preparing these in advance is essential. Make sure that they include open questions, allowing for understanding the meaning and significance of features or actions in the place of worship, rather than only closed questions looking for factual information. Be clear about ways in which the visit will be followed up back in the classroom, to build on learning.

Some key points to remember when visiting faith communities

In addition to any specific requirements, modest dress is the usual guideline. Shoes are removed before entering a mosque, mandir, gurdwara and Buddhist vihara. Check specific requirements when organising the visit.

The following practices are usual:

- **Mosque**

  Female: head, legs, arms covered

  Male: heads covered during prayer time

  Given Islamic emphasis on modesty, clothing should cover arms and legs. The rule is 'loose and concealing, not tight and revealing'. If possible, loose trousers should be worn.

- **Gurdwara**

  Female: head and legs covered

  Male: head covered

  No cigarettes are to be taken into the gurdwara.

Photographs: many places of worship will allow photographs to be taken at the appropriate time but prior permission should be sought.

Behaviour: normal good behaviour standards are appropriate. In all places of worship it would be disrespectful to chew, talk loudly, run around or touch things without invitation. In places where sitting on a carpeted floor is usual, it is disrespectful to sit with legs open and feet towards the focal point e.g. a deity, a holy book, mihrab, etc.

Hospitality: a number of places of worship will show hospitality to visitors by offering food or refreshment. It is important to prepare pupils for this. For example:

- Mandir: prashad – this may take the form of crystal sugar, almonds, sweets or snack food. It is not sacred and should be accepted with thanks and eaten on the spot.

- Gurdwara: kara prashad – a semi-solid cold food made from butter, semolina, sugar and milk, or a cup of tea boiled with milk. This is not a sacred food and should be accepted with thanks. Kara prashad can be kept for eating later.

Donations: places of worship do not, as a rule, charge for visits, but a donation is recommended.

Guidance for faith and belief visitors going into schools

Schools are plural communities. There may be pupils from a range of faith and belief traditions, and from a range of denominations within these; there may be many pupils from no particular faith background. Schools can provide rich opportunities for pupils by welcoming visitors from local religious and non-religious communities. Some schools remain hesitant about this, so this Code of Conduct is offered to encourage good relations between schools and visitors, and to make the most of the opportunity.

Code of Conduct

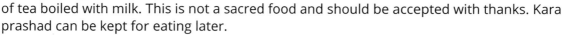
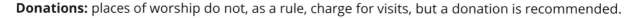

Religious visitors taking part in the life of a school should:

- be willing to share their own experiences, beliefs and insights, but avoid (a) criticism of the experience and insights of others and (b) imposing their views on pupils in any way

- be familiar with the school's aims, ethos and policies, and plan their involvement in the light of the aims and curriculum at the school. It is more effective to take part in the regular programme of teaching and learning rather than make an isolated or one-off contribution

- seek to use engaging teaching and learning methods that involve the pupils actively, and to communicate at appropriate levels for the age group(s) concerned. The most common problem for pupils when visitors make a classroom contribution is that they have to listen to a lengthy monologue that they can't understand because the material presented is too hard or the language is over the pupils' heads. Visitors who avoid these two pitfalls will be more effective

- make clear to pupils who they are, who they represent and what they are offering to the pupils during their visit

- be willing to respect and value the faith and belief of children and young people when it is different from their own

- develop ways of speaking to children that communicate an open approach, avoiding any hidden agenda to convert young people.

One question that may help visitors reflect on their approach in the classroom is: 'If a member of another religion or belief visited my child's school and contributed in the same way that I have done, would I, as a parent, be happy with the education given?'

A more detailed form of this information is available on the NATRE website and can be found at bit.ly/1Fj6pHr

RE, Citizenship and PSHE: what are the links?

RE provides many opportunities for pupils to develop social and interpersonal skills and to increase their understanding of human relationships and responsibilities within society. In these and other ways RE can make a significant contribution to Citizenship and PSHE.

Provision for RE should be clearly identifiable and distinct from other curriculum areas. It is important, however, to recognise that productive links may be made between RE, PSHE and Citizenship, both in content and approaches to learning, and that RE can make a substantial contribution to pupils' development both personally and as young citizens.

When planning the curriculum, schools need to ensure that RE is not driven by PSHE or Citizenship objectives. It must be planned in accordance with the RE syllabus, with RE learning objectives paramount.

The table below indicates some of the ways in which RE can contribute.

Some aspects of PSHE and Citizenship	RE provides opportunities for pupils to:
Health and well-being	
This concerns helping pupils lead confident, healthy and responsible lives as individuals and members of society, gaining practical knowledge and skills to help them live healthily and deal with the spiritual, moral, social and cultural issues they face as they mature.	• develop understanding and awareness of beliefs and values and how these motivate and guide actions at individual and community level • gain knowledge and understanding about the place and value of the individual, including insights of religions and beliefs about mind, body and – for some – soul or spirit.
Relationships	
This concerns helping pupils to recognise and develop healthy emotions and healthy relationships; the importance of commitment in relationships; issues of identity and diversity, including ways of working with others to challenge stereotypes and solve disputes.	• gain knowledge and understanding of beliefs, practices and lifestyles at local and national level, and how these are lived out in communities • develop knowledge and understanding of the beliefs and commitments of others • reflect on the values and intentions that underpin human actions.
Living in the wider world	
This concerns enabling pupils to develop attitudes of respect for themselves and those who see the world in a different way to themselves; to recognise and value equality in diverse communities; promoting dialogue between pupils about issues of belief, identity, community and religion; dealing with issues of social justice, interdependence, peace and conflict and sustainable development.	• develop knowledge, understanding and respect for different religious beliefs, values, traditions and ethical life stances • explore issues of rights, equality, justice, prejudice and discrimination, and the religious teachings and responses to these issues.
Rights and responsibilities of citizens	
This concerns enabling pupils to develop respect and understanding between the diverse communities and identities of the UK and beyond, including religious identities; to develop their own role in contributing to a vibrant society; and to develop understanding of the moral, not just the monetary, value of wealth.	• reflect on how humans treat each other and their environment • explore beliefs and teachings of world faiths on the origin and value of life, questions of identity and belonging, and matters of identity and purpose, from religious and non-religious traditions and communities.

A contribution to good assessment practice in RE through eight steps

In RE, by the end of each key stage, pupils are expected to know, apply and understand the matters, skills and processes specified in the RE programme of study, as in all subjects of the curriculum. The expectation is that pupils' achievements will be weighed up by teachers using criteria arising from the programmes of study. This statement is included in the programmes of study for each subject of the English National Curriculum, 2013.

All schools have a curriculum and assessment framework for all subjects that meets the set of core principles offered by the Department for Education (DfE). For RE assessment, like other subjects, you should use the outcomes for RE from your locally agreed syllabus, diocesan guidelines etc. (see p.4 on where you need to look). Subject leaders for RE should plan careful and progressed ways of describing achievement and progress for all pupils. The pages that follow offer teachers an 'eight steps up' approach to assessing RE. This offers a way forward from the eight-level scales often used in recent years, using new structures, but maintaining good continuity with past practice.

The core principles are that assessment should:

- set out clear learning steps so that pupils can reach or exceed the expected outcomes for each age group in RE
- enable teachers to measure whether pupils are on track to meet end-of-key-stage outcomes at key points, e.g. when reporting annually to parents on progress and achievement in RE, as the law requires
- enable teachers to pinpoint any aspects of the RE curriculum in which pupils are falling behind, and also to recognise exceptional performance
- support teachers' planning for progress in RE for all pupils
- enable the teacher to report regularly to parents and, when pupils move to other schools, provide clear information about each pupil's strengths, weaknesses and progress towards the end-of-key-stage outcomes.

In the light of these DfE principles and in relation to RE, this approach to assessing RE offers answers to five key questions.

1 What steps within an assessment framework enable pupils to reach or exceed the end-of-key-stage outcomes in the RE curriculum?

In RE, at 7, 11 and 14, pupils should show that they know, apply and understand the matters, skills and processes specified in the programme of study. Specific RE outcomes should guide teaching and learning.

The key concepts of RE: to be understood and applied

Good RE programmes of study enable pupils to increase and deepen their knowledge and understanding of key concepts in RE. These concepts relate to the religions and worldviews studied. The key concepts that make up RE's field of enquiry can be described like this:

- beliefs, teachings, sources of wisdom and authority
- experiences and ways of living
- ways of expressing meaning
- questions of identity, diversity and belonging
- questions of meaning, purpose and truth
- questions of values and commitments.

While this list of concepts bears a close relation to previous versions of RE curriculum guidance (e.g. the QCA National Non-statutory RE Framework of 2004), the concepts are listed here to provide a checklist of areas in which pupils will make progress towards outcomes in RE and to guide subject leaders in developing appropriate statements of attainment for different groups of pupils. They feature in many locally agreed syllabuses and are woven through the 2013 Framework for RE (see pp.3, 6–7).

Gaining and deploying skills

RE also sets ambitions for pupils' skills to be developed and seeks to assess progress in learning skills across the 5–14 age range. These skills are not developed in abstract, but always in relation to the religions and worldviews pupils study. As a result, pupils are increasingly enabled to develop both their knowledge and understanding and their expression and communication through the skills they gain and deploy.

While the outcomes of the programme of study make clear the skills that are expected of learners at the end of each key stage, you will need to plan programmes of study carefully to enable pupils to make progress towards these outcomes.

RE's aims for progression in understanding, expression of ideas and skills are made explicit in the three summary pyramid diagrams on p.60. These are presented for you to consider as you approach for yourself the tasks of describing progression in RE and designing lessons, tasks or tests that will enable fair, valid and manageable assessment for learning in RE. The pyramids relate closely to the three areas of aims for RE from the 2013 Framework for RE (see p.3).

② How can teachers and schools monitor and measure whether pupils are on track to meet end-of-key-stage expectations and outcomes?

- Some schools and subject leaders will use practice arising from the eight-level scales in use in RE over many years. Others may develop their practice in line with whole-school initiatives (examples include PIXL learning approaches, SOLO taxonomy or applications of Bloom's taxonomy). Usually, it is helpful to show progress in a larger number of smaller steps, rather than in great leaps! Through each key stage, progress can be described using the 'big steps' of the pyramids on pp.60–63, related to smaller steps that connect to particular content in units of study or investigations.

- Other schools and subject leaders will find the progression pyramids are a useful guide to thinking and planning comprehensively and developing pupils' skills across the range of RE's aims.

- It is important that RE assessment addresses all that pupils gain from the subject appropriately. The skills of investigation or reflection on meaning are as important as the acquisition of knowledge and enable pupils to deepen their thinking and build towards a coherent understanding of this knowledge across the subject.

- The new National Curriculum of 2013 and the end of the use of levels in the curriculum dealt with some long-standing RE assessment problems (over-assessment, excessive complexity, inaccurate and unfair assessment, the mistaken implication that progress in learning is linear). New assessment structures, devised by schools, should aim for simplicity, manageability and clarity for users – including pupils and parents.

③ How can teachers of RE pinpoint aspects of the curriculum where pupils may be falling behind, and also recognise exceptional performance?

- **Assessment for learning:** subject leaders and teachers should establish good practice in assessment for learning for each age group, in ways that enable all pupils (from those with SEN to gifted and talented pupils) to show their achievements clearly, so that next steps in learning can be planned appropriately for every child. Feedback to target improvement is most important.

- **Differentiation:** subject leaders and teachers should plan RE in the light of the fact that some pupils need to work below or above the outcomes expected for their age group in order to make the best progress possible in the subject. They may be working towards a step, achieving the step, or exceeding what the step requires. Along with many schools, you may find the framework of 'emerging, achieving, exceeding' a useful way of recording different outcomes in a class.

④ How can the descriptions of expectations for the end of each key stage in RE support teachers' planning for all pupils?

- **Using the learning outcomes:** subject leaders and teachers in RE should plan their approach to the whole key stage with the learning outcomes for the end of the key stage in clear view. Only where teachers are paying close attention to end-of-key stage outcomes throughout the stage can pupils work towards their highest possible achievements.

- **Setting high expectations early in the key stage:** in terms of the matters, skills and processes of RE, work that challenges pupils to aim for the end-of-key-stage outcomes early in their programmes of study is most likely to enable all pupils to reach the highest possible standards.

- **Planning progression step by step:** clear planning by subject leaders and teachers needs to deepen knowledge and understanding, to enable expression and communication and to recognise the skills pupils gain and deploy in studying religions and worldviews. Good programmes of learning and assessment describe clear steps that lead towards to the end of key stage achievements and outcomes.

- **Knowing what pupils already understand and can do:** a coherent approach across a key stage is vital to ensure progression. The starting point for any class teacher must be to establish and understand clearly what pupils already know, including any misconceptions they might have, in relation to the outcomes. Once this is clear, teachers can plan to develop pupils' understanding towards the outcomes.

⑤ How can expectations for RE be used to report strengths and weaknesses of pupils' progress to parents, and to other schools and teachers upon transfer?

- As with all subjects of the curriculum, parents are entitled to an annual report that clearly describes the progress and achievement of each child in relation to the RE programme of study.

- Good RE reporting is individual, positive, criterion referenced, accurate and diagnostic.

- The clearer the end-of-key-stage outcomes, the easier it should be to be clear about whether pupils are 'emerging, achieving or exceeding' in relation to these outcomes.

Progress steps in RE for 5–14s

Eight steps in relation to the three aims of RE

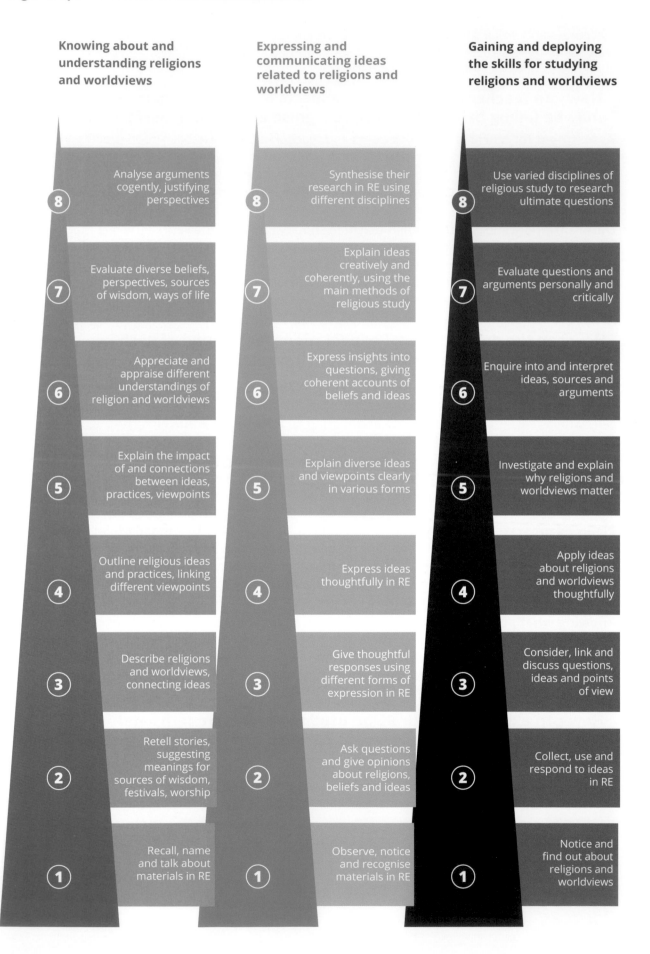

Knowing about and understanding religions and worldviews

8. Analyse arguments cogently, justifying perspectives
7. Evaluate diverse beliefs, perspectives, sources of wisdom, ways of life
6. Appreciate and appraise different understandings of religion and worldviews
5. Explain the impact of and connections between ideas, practices, viewpoints
4. Outline religious ideas and practices, linking different viewpoints
3. Describe religions and worldviews, connecting ideas
2. Retell stories, suggesting meanings for sources of wisdom, festivals, worship
1. Recall, name and talk about materials in RE

Expressing and communicating ideas related to religions and worldviews

8. Synthesise their research in RE using different disciplines
7. Explain ideas creatively and coherently, using the main methods of religious study
6. Express insights into questions, giving coherent accounts of beliefs and ideas
5. Explain diverse ideas and viewpoints clearly in various forms
4. Express ideas thoughtfully in RE
3. Give thoughtful responses using different forms of expression in RE
2. Ask questions and give opinions about religions, beliefs and ideas
1. Observe, notice and recognise materials in RE

Gaining and deploying the skills for studying religions and worldviews

8. Use varied disciplines of religious study to research ultimate questions
7. Evaluate questions and arguments personally and critically
6. Enquire into and interpret ideas, sources and arguments
5. Investigate and explain why religions and worldviews matter
4. Apply ideas about religions and worldviews thoughtfully
3. Consider, link and discuss questions, ideas and points of view
2. Collect, use and respond to ideas in RE
1. Notice and find out about religions and worldviews

Eight steps up: knowing about and understanding religions and worldviews

Examples: knowing and understanding

These examples of the knowledge and understanding pupils gain in RE need to be read in the light of the RE requirements for each key stage. The examples are just one illustration of the planned progression that pupils need.

8 — Analyse arguments cogently, justifying perspectives

Pupils use varied methods from sociology of religion to analyse the ways Christian, Muslim and Sikh population patterns and community life are changing in twenty-first-century Britain and their local area. They justify their perspectives on whether and how a plural society can be built peacefully.

7 — Evaluate diverse beliefs, perspectives, sources of wisdom, ways of life

Pupils weigh up debates and arguments between agnostics, Christians and Muslims about diverse ideas of God, using philosophical methods. They evaluate the arguments of others in relation to their own ideas and viewpoints, using skills of personal and impersonal evaluation.

6 — Appreciate and appraise different understandings of religion and worldviews

Pupils argue for their answer to the question 'Would an omnipresent God need special places for people to worship?' They examine the architecture of mosques, cathedrals and gurdwaras in the UK today, developing their appreciation and appraisal of forms and functions of varied places of worship.

5 — Explain the impact of and connections between ideas, practices, viewpoints

Pupils explain the impact that religious and/or spiritual experiences have had on some people from 'eyewitness' accounts. They give their reasons for accepting or rejecting some explanations – including psychological and theological – of these events.

4 — Outline religious ideas and practices, linking different viewpoints

Pupils consider some different possible meanings for two parables of Jesus and what the parables mean to Christians today. They rank the possible interpretations, giving a reason why they consider one to be a better interpretation than another.

3 — Describe religions and worldviews, connecting ideas

Pupils select their favourite two or three 'wise sayings' from ten examples drawn from different sources (Bible, Qur'an, Torah, Dhammapada) and illustrate these sayings. They describe what each religion teaches in relation to the sayings. They describe connections between the sayings they have chosen.

2 — Retell stories, suggesting meanings for sources of wisdom, festivals, worship

Pupils enact two stories. Examples could be parts of the story of Holy Week and Easter, and parts of the Diwali story. They discuss the ideas and characters and suggest what the stories mean.

1 — Recall, name and talk about materials in RE

Pupils discover how Muslims wash, bow and pray in a daily pattern, for example, learning the word wudu/wuzu. They name the religion and the word Muslims use for washing and talk about what happens and what it might mean.

Eight steps up: expressing and communicating ideas relating to religions and worldviews

Examples: expressing and communicating

These examples of the communication and expression pupils learn in RE need to be read in the light of the RE requirements for each key stage. The examples are just one illustration of the planned progression that pupils need.

8 Synthesise their research in RE using different disciplines

Pupils consider the questions: 'Is Buddhism a religion?' 'In what ways is Humanism like a religion?' They bring together their research into the two questions, evaluating arguments about the nature of religions and worldviews critically. They answer for themselves: 'Why are you religious, or not religious?'

7 Explain ideas creatively and coherently, using the main methods of religious stduy

Pupils give coherent and thoughtful explanations of the thought and poetry of Primo Levi and Dietrich Bonhoeffer, religious thinkers persecuted under Nazism. They use historical, theological and philosophical methods to evaluate the question: 'Is it possible to believe in God after the Holocaust?'

6 Express insights into questions, giving coherent accounts of beliefs and ideas

Pupils express insights of their own in comparing the influence of Aung San Suu Kyi and of Revd Dr Martin Luther King. They give coherent accounts of the impact of ideas such as non-violence, pacifism and spiritual strength. They make coherent connections between Buddhist and Christian ideas, beliefs and practice and the influences they examine.

5 Explain diverse ideas and viewpoints clearly in various forms

Pupils are given eight quotations, four of which claim religion is a force for good, and four of which say it does more damage than good. They use the ideas to explain their viewpoint about the question 'Is religion a force for good or not?'

4 Express ideas thoughtfully in RE

Pupils express thoughtful ideas about the Five Pillars of Islam, applying the general concepts of devotion to God, service of other people and self-discipline to Muslim practice. They give thoughtful ideas of their own about the value of the practices.

3 Give thoughtful responses using different forms of expression in RE

Pupils discuss three religious artworks from three different centuries, considering what inspired these artists to create great religious work. They respond by choosing examples of religious art that they find inspiring. They create expressions of their own ideas.

2 Ask questions and give opinions about religions, beliefs and ideas

Pupils take part in a music session using songs about peace from different religions. They ask questions and say what they like about the songs' words, and what is important about peace to them.

1 Observe, notice and recognise materials in RE

Pupils watch a video of some interesting festivities at Diwali and Easter and ask 'Who, What, When, How, Why?' questions about what they have seen.

Eight steps up: gaining and deploying the skills needed to enquire into religions and worldviews

Examples: gaining and deploying skills

These examples of the skills of religious study that pupils gain and deploy in RE need to be read in the light of your RE requirements for each key stage. The examples are just one illustration of the planned progression in learning that pupils need.

Step	Skill	Example
8	Use varied disciplines of religious study to research ultimate questions	Pupils use ideas and methods from theology, philosophy and psychology to research varied answers to questions about God, discovering and expressing arguments from different viewpoints comprehensively.
7	Evaluate questions and arguments personally and critically	Pupils evaluate research that finds religious people are happier than non-religious people, asking: 'Can this be proved?' 'What evidence is there?' 'What explanations are there?' 'Does this finding offer evidence in favour of religion, or does it merely imply that illusions can be comforting?'
6	Enquire into and interpret ideas, sources and arguments	Pupils plan an enquiry into identity: why do millions of people identify themselves as atheists, Christians or Muslims in Britain today? They communicate their interpretations of the worldviews of others accurately.
5	Investigate and explain why religions and worldviews matter	Pupils investigate questions about life after death, explaining varied answers, using concepts like consciousness, soul, moksha or Paradise. They explain the impact of varied views about life after death on life today, expressing ideas about destiny reasonably, creatively and thoughtfully.
4	Apply ideas about religions and worldviews thoughtfully	Pupils hear the stories of the enlightenment of the Buddha, of the giving of the Qur'an in Islam and of the birth of Jesus in Christianity. They consider what members of these religions believe these stories to show. They learn the word 'revelation' and apply the idea to the stories. They discuss what it means to believe in revelation.
3	Consider, link and discuss questions, ideas and points of view	Pupils consider and discuss examples of what key leaders from stories in two different faiths have done to make peace. They raise questions about peacemaking, giving thoughtful ideas of their own on the question: 'Would you like to be a peacemaker?'
2	Collect, use and respond to ideas in RE	Pupils collect examples of living together happily both from school life and from religious stories. They offer ideas of their own to be included in a 'recipe for living together happily'.
1	Notice and find out about religions and worldviews	Pupils show curiosity about what Muslims, or Jews or Christians do each day or each week. They notice some details that interest them and find out more.

Picturing progress and achievement

This material aims to enable you to think clearly and plan well for progression in RE learning. It uses the outcomes from the 2013 RE Council's Curriculum Framework for RE (see pp.3, 6–7), which are expressed here as progressing steps. There are strong connections with wider curriculum work, such as approaches using Bloom's taxonomy of thinking. Each example of core knowledge in RE is illustrated with increasingly challenging tasks. Outcomes are expressed in relation to one or two of the steps that have been discussed on pages 57–63. These progression grids give ideas for learning that target increasing knowledge and understanding, creative enquiry, and the gaining and deployment of the skills pupils need to study religions and beliefs.

The examples give practical lesson ideas for some commonly taught topics with examples from different religions and beliefs. It is always important to set the learning in the context of shared human experience (e.g. of celebrating, of memory, of community life, of belief about God) and to link the beliefs and values of the living religious traditions with the pupils' own senses of meaning and the search for meaning. Progress in RE is not like the straight lines of mathematics: children learn in complex, textured and multi-dimensional ways how religion works and what beliefs and values in life matter to whom.

Many of the outcomes are expressed in terms of pupil-friendly 'I can ...' statements. This does not mean that assessment is only through pupils' self-assessment. You and your school's other teachers of RE need to find ways of seeing whether pupils really *can* say 'I can ...' to these outcomes.

Example 1: simple progression in learning from Islamic and Christian festivals and celebrations – Ramadan and Eid-ul-Fitr and Christmas

The 'I can ...' statements here are derived from the outcomes for RE in the 2013 Framework (see pp.3, 6–7).

	These are not normative, but rather just examples of how to describe pupils' progress. However, they add content to the steps and are written to help inform teachers' planning.
Step 1	I can name Christmas and Eid-ul-Fitr and talk about special days in my own family and community, noticing and recognising religious features.
Step 2	I can retell a story of the giving of the Qur'an or of the birth of Jesus. I can respond sensitively to a moment or character in the story for myself, collecting simple ideas and suggesting meanings for aspects of the story.
Step 3	I can describe what happens at Eid in a mosque, or at Christmas in a church. I can give thoughtful responses that link this up to some feelings and experiences that I share on 'big days' in my family life (e.g. feeling joyful, feeling excited, feeling sad, feeling togetherness, remembering, being generous).
Step 4	I can outline the meaning of words like 'celebrate,' 'messenger', 'miracle' or 'revelation'. I can apply the idea of celebration and/or revelation to two religions and to my own life, developing my own reasonable ideas about questions such as 'What's worth celebrating today?' or 'How do religious stories of revelation make a difference to people's lives?'
Step 5	I can explain why Eid and Christmas are similar in some ways, and explain three differences between them (explaining diversity). I can explain my viewpoint about whether religious people in the UK should be given a day off work for a major festival, in the light of religious teaching, giving some reasons and examples.
Step 6	I can interpret some sources and meanings of two festivals for myself, referring to quotations from sacred texts directly (e.g. hadith, gospel), expressing insights of my own. I can appreciate and appraise the significance of celebration in religions, interpreting the varied impacts of faith: what could anyone learn from Muslims and Christians about celebration? Does everyone need to celebrate something? Why is this? What arguments are there against my views?
Step 7	I can give creative and varied explanations of some ways Christmas has become a kind of 'plural festival' and how 'British Eid' is different from Eid in Pakistan or Egypt. I can evaluate, personally and impersonally/critically, the reasons why festivals are the most popular parts of a religious life. Examples from Christianity and Islam: Why do more people go to church at Christmas? Why is Eid so important and widely celebrated in British Islam? What would a sociologist say about this?
Step 8	I can analyse different points of view about festivals using both sociological and theological ideas and being alert to the contexts of religious celebration. I can justify my view about whether non-believers should join in with religious festivals or not, bringing my research together effectively.

You might think about this grid in relation to the following questions:

- What links would work on these skills offer to some of the other subjects of the curriculum? (These links might be to literacy, science, citizenship, history, arts and more.)
- Do the advantages of making these links outweigh the threat of RE getting 'lost' or getting 'watered down'?
- In what ways do pupils benefit from assessment approaches like this one? Do teachers benefit? (Is it simpler than levelling?)

Example 2: progressed tasks on the topic of sacred spaces

In this example, the kinds of tasks teachers set to enable pupils to show progress are the focus. You might like to construct a grid like this using the steps, addressing another key area of RE knowledge. Sacred space is a suitable focus for this example because it is a topic to be studied at increasing depth: it is possible to continue beyond Step 8 as far as a PhD within this area of understanding!

	Teaching and learning activity *These suggestions, often with a literacy link, offer just one way to approach the achievements. There are many more.*	Outcomes related to steps *These are in teacher-language, but can be translated into pupil-language of 'I can ...'*
Step 1	Show pupils a range of 'special places' in pictures and by a visit. Ask them to think about the Jewish festival of Sukkot, where Jewish people live in the outdoors, like camping in the garden. What would it be like? In teams, ask the children to make some sukkah, or dens, like the Jewish ones. Can they enjoy some food together in their sukkah? Watch out for signs of achievement in their teamwork and conversation. Talk about these questions.	**Early Learning Goals (ELGs): understanding the world – cultures and beliefs** Children begin to know about their own cultures and beliefs and those of Jewish people. **ELGs: personal, social and emotional development, self-confidence and self-esteem** Children have a developing awareness of their own needs, views and feelings and become more sensitive to those of others.
Step 1–2	Pupils use images of a mosque or a church to talk about, name and identify features of the sacred buildings of Muslims or Christians. They make lists, labels and simple captions for features of the places of worship (a strong literacy link). They talk about what happens inside: music, eating, sharing, friendship, praying. Which matters most, do they think? How does it feel inside? What do people say about their holy building?	**Step 1:** Pupils talk about their labels, lists and captions of things we might see in a church or mosque, identifying simple features. **Step 2:** Pupils suggest meanings for some of the symbols and objects in a church or a mosque, and some actions people perform there.
Step 1–2	Pupils, having visited a place of worship, recount their trip using photographs they took while there. They create, as a team, a six-page guide booklet about the place they visited, using their own photos of six important things they learned. They write poems of feelings that reflect the building's atmosphere and worship.	**Step 1:** Pupils identify some key features of the place visited and talk about what they think they are used for. **Step 2:** Pupils suggest meanings for different things they found out about in a place of worship and respond sensitively to what the atmosphere was like, in the form of a poem.
Step 3–4	Pupils raise their own questions about holy buildings, then use pictures and video clips to find out about worship in a mosque and church (or two other settings). They make lists of what happens, using the right words, and consider the questions: What is similar in both places? What is unique to each place? How do these buildings show what Christians and Muslims believe about God, praying, worship or community life?	**Step 3:** Pupils describe key features of two religious buildings, making a simple comparison between them. They look for signs of what is valued highly in two places of worship, and discuss similarities and differences between these values. **Step 4:** Pupils use some key concepts of religion (God, belief, prayer, community) to show how much they understand about Muslim and Christian worship.

Step 3–4

Pupils consider what places of worship there are in the local area. They research this information using directories and online guides. How many churches, mosques or mandirs in their town can they find on the web? Can they find out when they were built or opened? Is their area typical of Britain, or unusual in some ways? What is good about living in a country where people from many different religions and worldviews share towns and cities? They prepare a report on 'sacred space in our community', giving facts and ideas about their findings and the issues they have encountered.

Step 3: Pupils describe the religious make-up of the area in relation to another area of the country; they make links between their area and another area, perhaps more or less pluralist. Pupils say what they think about living in a country where people from many religions share towns and cities (this task links to the Geography curriculum).

Step 4: Pupils use the right words and concepts to apply their learning: what will happen to the numbers of religious buildings in our community in 10 or 50 years' time? What factors will make a difference?

Step 3–4

Pupils rank a list of activities that happen in a mosque or a church: praying/washing/helping homeless people/teaching children about the faith/socialising/celebrating/reading and discussing the scriptures/worshipping/welcoming school visits/singing/debating/doing charitable work/celebrating festivals. They respond to questions: Which matter most, and which matter least? To whom? Why?

Step 3: Pupils describe the practices of two different religious communities, identifying the impact of each religion's teaching on what the community does.

Step 4: Pupils apply ideas of their own about what matters most in a mosque or church to the ranking task and the explanations that follow, giving reasons for the ideas they agree with.

Step 4–5

Pupils use a 'Shall we sell the church?' activity role play to explore and consider a dilemma for a contemporary Christian community that has grown smaller and write a persuasive text (literacy links) explaining, with reasons, what they think about the dilemma: should a shrinking community sell its building and use the money for goodness? They engage with a range of biblical texts about what matters in the Christian community. Teaching encourages them to use RE-specific vocabulary like the 'mission of the church', 'worship', 'sacred', 'community', as well as words like 'dilemma' and 'compromise'.

Step 4: Pupils apply their own ideas to thinking about how a community responds to declining numbers and the mission of the church. Pupils show that they understand the significance of worship, charity and community to Christians.

Step 5: Pupils express clear and well-informed views on how a Christian community could put its mission into action, explaining reasons thoughtfully.

Step 5–6

Small teams of pupils are challenged: design a multi-faith worship space for an airport, prison, shopping centre or school that expresses creatively solutions to some interfaith issues and questions

Write an explanation of the issues around interfaith worship and explain reasons for their sensitivity: religions are many, but is God one? Do the faiths share more than they differ on? Would an inclusive holy building leave anyone out – what about atheists and people who are spiritual but not religious?

Step 5: Pupils investigate and explain some examples of diversity in religious worship.

They explain why sharing worship space is a very sensitive issue for believers in different communities and communicate their ideas in their design.

Step 6: Pupils appreciate and appraise different views about worship and shared sacred space. Pupils interpret different viewpoints about whether shared worship is a good idea, or even a possibility, exploring the idea 'religions are many, even if God is one'.

Step 6	There are over 1700 mosques and over 30,000 churches in the UK: how does this compare with another country? What does it show and imply about religion in Britain today: will it grow stronger or die out?	**Step 6:** Pupils appreciate and appraise the changing religious landscape of the UK and argue with good reasons for their point of view on the question 'Will religion grow stronger or die out in the future?'
Step 7	Pupils generate and evaluate arguments on both sides of these quotations, using sophisticated reasoning: 'If the church really wanted to follow Jesus, it would sell its buildings and use the money charitably.' 'If Muslims expressed the true spirit of Islam they would not build new mosques, but would spend their money to rescue the starving children of the world.'	**Step 7:** Pupils evaluate arguments on both sides of the debate about whether alleviating poverty is the first or only duty of religions. Pupils give varied creative and critical evaluations of the ways religions use their resources.
Step 8	Pupils research some ancient and modern examples of creative design in churches and mosques, studying what makes a sacred space from theological, sociological and personal viewpoints. They propose architect's guidelines for building sacred spaces in the twenty-first century, justifying their ideas fully.	**Step 8:** Pupils synthesise their research into places of worship and their meanings from different religions, using different disciplines of religious study to justify their own ideas about the significance of sacred space in the twenty-first century.

Example 3: an assessment for learning progression example – learning from the art of the life of Jesus

This work uses a template for pupils to express their learning from Jesus and art. In order to integrate assessment of the three aims for RE from the 2013 Framework (see p.3), expressed in the three pyramids (see p.60), this strategy asks seventeen carefully planned questions about the links and connections between the pupil and the work he or she has done on art and the life of Jesus. They are all about the skills of reflecting, engaging and responding. They do not test factual recall, although they do rely upon pupils knowing a lot of stuff about Jesus, and they require pupils to use that understanding.

Knowledge and understanding

The task helps pupils to demonstrate knowledge and understanding, connecting ideas, beliefs, teachings and sources of wisdom with global forms of Christian expression.

Expression and communication

This task enables a wide range of creative, enquiring and thoughtful ideas to be expressed in pupil-centred ways.

Gaining and deploying RE skills

The task gives pupils the chance to develop skills of self-expression, application of ideas, interpretation of texts and evaluation of forms of religious expression in progressed ways. They are encouraged to respond reasonably to the religious material they encounter.

The seventeen questions are provocative and aim to enable pupils to apply their own ideas, express their views and develop insight. Usually, pupils are asked to select four out of the seventeen questions offered and answer only these. The task has strong elements of spiritual and cultural development: the questions often demand that pupils think for themselves, apply their understanding, and use their own experience and insight in developing their answers.

The task enables you to practise the best elements of assessment for learning in RE by, for example:

- **Choice:** giving pupils an individually chosen route through the task. Research shows that chosen tasks often reveal more accurately the best of what a student can do.
- **Self- and peer assessment:** the questions are not all equally difficult, so the choices pupils make and the process of drafting and redrafting answers in discussion leads to increasing self-awareness among pupils. Ask them to compare their draft answers with a partner and help each other to improve for a good peer assessment activity.
- **Sharing assessment criteria with pupils:** all aspects of the activity have tailored mark schemes, showing the factors that enable a pupil to climb up a step. Sharing these mark schemes with pupils enables them to challenge themselves, and to aim high.
- **WILF ('What I'm looking for ...'):** the structure of the task and the mark scheme is intended to show the pupil clearly what you are looking for in the answers.

Jesus and art: choose four from the question bank

In this assessment activity, you have seventeen questions to choose from and you need to answer four of these. Look at all seventeen and discuss with a partner which four you will choose. Don't do those that look easiest – aim to demonstrate how much you have learned about the life, teachings and significance of Jesus.

When you have chosen them, write a clear, considered answer to each of the four questions. Give as much thoughtful insight of your own as you can. You may add a sketch or image to your work if it helps to make your point.

1. What is the best work of art inspired by the life of Jesus you have seen? Explain your answer, give reasons, and talk in terms of its emotional impact.

2. List and explain three things you think would be satisfying for a Christian artist in a particular country of the world.

3. List three or more of the hard things about being a Christian artist today. Explain why you chose these three.

4. If you could be a journalist and interview Jesus for a magazine, which magazine would you choose and why? What four questions would you ask? How do you think he would answer?

5. Christians think Jesus is one of the top leaders ever – actually God on earth, incarnate in human form. What made him so brilliant at what he did?

6. What similarities and differences between Jesus and another inspiring human (choose your own) can you see? Explain your lists.

7. Artists from all over the world often paint Jesus as a person from their own culture. Why? Is this effective?

8. Christians seek to live a life of love and to be changed by the Spirit of God. How do you think the faith helps people to find 'the way, the truth and the life'? What sort of way, truth or life is this?

9. 'Creating a work of art is an act of worship for me.' What does the artist who says this mean? Give your own definition of art and worship. Are they similar?

10. Christians believe that God can help you find the path for true living. What do you think is the way to find the path for true living? How does this compare with a Christian path?

11. Christians say they get strength, direction and purpose from the Bible. How? What gives you strength or direction in life? Where does your sense of purpose come from? Compare this with a Christian viewpoint.

12. Christianity is two thousand years old and has over two billion followers – a third of the world's population. It's the biggest religion in the world. Explain what you think accounts for its success.

13. 'Turn from your old life and put your trust in Jesus,' say Christians. What do they mean? If you were asked for your formula to change the world for the better, what would you say? Give at least three reasons to explain your answer.

14. What do you think are the three most important things you have learned about Christian art in this work?

15. 'The cross is a reminder of where human evil was worst – but the love of Jesus won.' This is an explanation of Christianity's common symbol, the cross. What do you think a cross means to a Christian? Comment on how different artists use the symbol of the cross.

16. If you became a Christian, what would be easy and what would be hard for you? (Don't answer this question if you are a Christian: try number 17 instead!)

17. If you are a Christian, make a list of the differences between what you learned in RE and what you learned from your family or church about your faith this year.

Assessing the outcomes of this work

You can work at Step 3 if you can say 'yes' to most of these …	• I can say what I think about some examples of Christian art. • I can describe some Christian beliefs simply. • I can discuss and consider questions about Christianity and art. • I can make some links between stories of Jesus and works of art for myself.
You can work at Step 4 if you can say 'yes' to most of these …	• I can develop ideas about art and Jesus for myself. • I can make some sense of two works of art about Jesus. • I can apply the ideas of 'Incarnation', 'Saviour', 'Lord' or 'Rabbi' to examples of the portrayal of Jesus in art. • I can outline some of the reasons why Jesus is a figure of worship across the world. • I can refer to the teaching of the Bible in showing what I understand about how art works. • I can say what Christians value and why.
You can work at Step 5 if you can say 'yes' to most of these …	• I can investigate what's most important to Christians, and to me, saying why. • I can explain the impact of art about Jesus thoughtfully, for myself. • I can explain why two Christian artists give diverse expressions of the same idea or story. • I can explain how and why varied Christian experience in different countries is reflected in art. • I can explore and express thoughtful views of my own about art as worship.
You can work at Step 6 if you can say 'yes' to most of these …	• I can interpret gospel writing in the light of the work of some Christian artists. • I can appreciate and appraise key Christian beliefs about Jesus as leader, Saviour or Lord and argue for my own ideas about his status. • I can interpret the significance of symbols in Christian art and respond insightfully myself. • I can express my own insights into the life and teaching of Jesus in a work of art and talk thoughtfully about my work. • I can explain clearly a Christian perspective on values and what matters most. • I can relate my own views of life to Christian teaching and ideas expressed in art.
You can work at Step 7 if you can say 'yes' to most of these …	• I can evaluate Christian artistic expressions about the life of Jesus Christ, both personally and critically. • I can use evidence and examples to explain clearly and in detail what I think about key aspects of Christianity expressed artistically. • I can give creative and varied explanations of Christian commitments and of my own commitments. • I can evaluate Christian artistic expressions about life's meaning and purpose with evidence and examples, in relation to my own ideas.

Learning is a complex process, as, of course, is teaching. It is not possible to capture this complexity in a few pages of a book. There is not always strong evidence from research for some classroom practices. Where there is evidence, it needs to be taken with caveats that many factors are involved in aiming to help pupils learn and make progress, so it is not possible to single out individual factors with confidence.

Having said that, substantial research does suggest the following:

(1) Teachers who have good subject knowledge, and who are able to understand the misconceptions of pupils in understanding that knowledge, can have a strong impact on pupils' outcomes.[33] However, subject knowledge in itself is not the most important factor, but being able to organise and *use* this knowledge in ways that enable pupils to access and appropriate it.[34]

(2) In order to develop competence in a subject, pupils need to have a good foundation of factual knowledge, be able to understand facts and ideas in the context of a wider conceptual framework, and organise knowledge so that they can recall and apply it to new contexts.[35] Daniel Willingham calls this 'shallow' and 'deep' learning. Teaching must use 'shallow' to be able to build up 'deep' learning.

(3) Teachers who teach in order to enable the above can have a strong impact on pupils' achievement. They do this through the quality of their instructions, such as use of effective questioning and assessment to establish pupils' understanding, practice of skills and processes, modelling expected responses and scaffolding new learning.[36] Fundamental to this approach is a use of feedback in a formative way.[37]

So, recognising that it is easier to write about these things than it is to put them into practice, here is one strategy that pulls together some of these key features, together with some examples of how it might apply to RE.

Planning for progress: SOLO taxonomy

This approach, based on the work of John Biggs and Kevin Collis,[38] fits in well with the need for 'shallow' learning before 'deep' learning can take place. It allows for teachers to make use of effective questioning, formative feedback etc. It leaves space for teachers to get to grips with pupils' misconceptions en route to achieving clear outcomes.

The taxonomy looks at the structure of the *content* pupils need to learn (rather than focusing on the skills, as in Bloom's taxonomy). It looks like this.

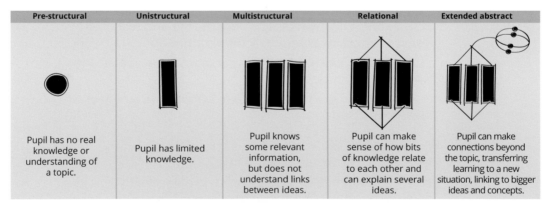

Pre-structural	Unistructural	Multistructural	Relational	Extended abstract
Pupil has no real knowledge or understanding of a topic.	Pupil has limited knowledge.	Pupil knows some relevant information, but does not understand links between ideas.	Pupil can make sense of how bits of knowledge relate to each other and can explain several ideas.	Pupil can make connections beyond the topic, transferring learning to a new situation, linking to bigger ideas and concepts.

The next pages offer a model planning sheet and some examples to explain how this taxonomy might support pupil progress in understanding and skills in RE.

---

[33] Robert Coe et al., *What Makes Great Teaching?* (Sutton Trust 2014); MS Donovan et al., *How People Learn: Bridging Research and Practice* (National Academy Press 1999).

[34] John Hattie, *Visible Learning for Teachers* (Routledge 2012).

[35] Donovan et al., *How People Learn* (see footnote 33); Daniel Willingham, *Why Don't Students Like School?* (Jossey-Bass 2009).

[36] Coe et al., *What Makes Great Teaching?* (see footnote 33).

[37] Hattie, *Visible Learning for Teachers* (see footnote 34); Dylan Wiliam, *Embedded Formative Assessment* (Solution Tree Press 2011).

[38] John Biggs and Kevin Collis, *Evaluating the Quality of Learning: The Solo Taxonomy* (Academic Press 1982).

SOLO taxonomy planning sheet: just to get you started ...

- Where is this unit placed in your longer-term progression plan?
- What are you going to want your students to know/understand/be able to do by the end?

Key question for your unit: _____

Pre-structural	**What do students already know?** Every time we start a new topic, students' understanding will drop. Learning is more a series of lurches than smooth progress!	**How are you going to find this out?** Remember that understanding students' misconceptions is vital, and checking these needs to continue through the topic.
Unistructural	**Where are you going to start?**	**What activities will enable students to gain this knowledge/these skills?** Plan a variety of ways to get students to think hard so that they learn the key information they need to address the question. You will need to spend sufficient time to enable students to grasp the ideas, in preparation for the next stage.
Multistructural	**What are the key ideas students need to be able to make sense of this topic and answer your key question?**	
Relational	**Where and how are these ideas related to the key concept within your topic?** Of course, you can make simple connections or develop deeper ones.	**What activities will bring these ideas together in a coherent way?** A variety of activities is needed, requiring students to apply their learning from the previous stage, and to carry on thinking hard!
Extended abstract	**How can students make links with wider learning?** Don't underestimate how demanding this stage is. It is possible that younger pupils (up to age 9?) may not manage this at all. An easier step is to see how students can make links within the wider learning in RE, rather than beyond the subject. However, this can still be demanding.	**What activities will set a wider context to demonstrate that students really have understood the question and the preceding knowledge (and skills)?**

SOLO taxonomy planning sheet: primary example (for 7–9s)

Key question for your unit: How and why does the Holy Qur'an matter to Muslims?[39]

Pre-structural

What do students already know?
- Perhaps some understanding that some objects, including books, are special to people

How are you going to find out?
- Question-and-answer session; mix and match exercise – sorting names of holy books and which religion they belong to, etc.

Unistructural

Where are you going to start?
- The difference between something being 'special' and 'precious' and being 'sacred' and 'holy'

What activities will enable students to gain this knowledge/these skills?
- Introduce mystery object, wrapped in cloth: what might it be? How do you treat something that is precious?
- Reveal translation of Qur'an on stand; explore basic facts about the language and structure (chapters/surahs and verses/ayat); read some extracts e.g. Surah 1, Al-Fatihah; explore meaning
- Read the story about how the Prophet Muhammad received the revelation on the 'Night of Power'
- Read some comments from Muslims about what the Qur'an means to them
- Try out and devise some similes for the Qur'an ('It might be like an ocean because ... it is deep and can take a lifetime to explore')

Multistructural

What are the key ideas students need to be able to make sense of this topic and answer your key question?
- Holy Qur'an as sacred to Muslims
- The direct word of Allah received by Prophet Muhammad (pbuh) via Jibril, the 'Night of Power'
- Received and written in Arabic
- Surah 1, Al-Fatihah, contains 'the essence of the Qur'an'

Relational

Where and how are these ideas related to the key concept within your topic?
- How Muhammad faced some opposition but kept going
- Use ways Muslims celebrate to show how important the Qur'an is
- How Muslims use the Qur'an to guide their living

What activities will bring these ideas together in a coherent way?
- Explore the cost to Muhammad of bringing this message to the people of Makkah: why was it so important to keep going in the face of challenges?
- Find out how Muslims celebrate the giving of the Qur'an today. Why do they do this?
- Ask some Muslims how they use the Qur'an

Extended abstract

How can students make links with wider learning?
- Some people devote a lifetime to memorising the Qur'an – to become a hafiz/hafiza. What does this show about how important the Qur'an is to Muslims?
- Compare with other things that people devote their lives to; note the differences between pursuing a hobby or interest (which might make you a better runner, for example) and trying to follow a path laid down by God, which affects all parts of life.

What activities will set a wider context to demonstrate that students really have understood the question and the preceding knowledge (and skills)?
- Memorise a suitable class text, perhaps a poem or story. What are the challenges of learning this?
- What would it be like to memorise over 70,000 words in a language you don't speak?
- Compare how people put huge amounts of effort into the things that matter to them. Compare similarities and differences.

---

[39] For resources for this unit, see Fiona Moss, ed., *Opening Up RE: Islam* (RE Today 2010).

SOLO taxonomy planning sheet: secondary example (for 14–15s)

Key question for your unit: How and why is the Holy Spirit important for Christians?[40]

Pre-structural	**What do students already know?** • Basic ideas about God in Christianity, e.g. the term Trinity and its meaning	**How are you going to find out?** • Get students to write a 50-word paragraph explaining what they know and understand
Unistructural	**Where are you going to start?** • God: Father, Son and Holy Spirit	**What activities will enable students to gain this knowledge/these skills?** • Give introductory information sheet; read, devise questions for each other, answer them, order what matters most to Christians etc. • Use information to say what an artwork might need to include to convey ideas about the Holy Spirit • Look at other images and compare • Design their own image and explain how images, symbols and words convey Christian belief in and the role of the Holy Spirit
Multistructural	**What are the key ideas students need to be able to make sense of this topic and answer your key question?** • Trinity • the Holy Spirit as God's power in world • biblical terms and images • Pentecost • gifts and fruit of the Spirit in the Bible	
Relational	**Where and how are these ideas related to the key concept within your topic?** • See the impact that belief in the Holy Spirit has on how Christians live their everyday lives • Compare different responses within Christianity – charismatic, e.g. Pentecostal; non-charismatic, e.g. some Anglicans, Quakers, URC • Why do some see the 'gifts' as only for the time of early Church?	**What activities will bring these ideas together in a coherent way?** • Explore ways in which Christians use the gifts of the Spirit in the church and their lives today; similarities and differences • Explore how and why Christians want to develop the 'fruit' of the Spirit • Contextualise fruit within understanding of sin and grace • Comparison with motivation for developing these virtues beyond Christian worldview
Extended abstract	**How can students make links with wider learning?** How important is the Holy Spirit within Christianity? This requires an understanding of: • the distinctiveness of Christian belief about Trinity • the impact of belief in the Holy Spirit on daily Christian living • Christian ideas that they need to rely upon the Holy Spirit for ongoing 'sanctification'	**What activities will set a wider context to demonstrate that students really have understood the question and the preceding knowledge (and skills)?** Apply their learning to the key question: 'No Holy Spirit, no Christianity' – how far is this true? • Consider the importance of the Holy Spirit: if there were no belief in the Holy Spirit, what would Christianity be like? • Wider implications for religion and belief: if there's no God, what reasons/explanations are there for why religions persist? How plausible/persuasive are these to people and why?

[40] For resources for this unit, see Stephen Pett, ed., *Essential RE: Spirit* (RE Today 2015).

Religions and worldviews:
what do you need to know?

Teaching religions and beliefs

In the past 60 years, the nature and purpose of Religious Education have changed and developed. These changes can be broadly characterised as a move through the following approaches (in this simplified account):

- **Religious Knowledge or Religious Instruction**: essentially nurturing pupils into the Christian faith.
- **Religious Studies**: exploring the phenomena of religion as an academic discipline. Teachers and pupils put their own beliefs and assumptions to one side and explored the nature and impact of religion on believers. The content of the curriculum reflected a systematic study within a structure of comparative religion.
- **Religious Education**: an educational project as part of a secular education system. The curriculum is developed on the basis of what supports the human development of children and young people. The widespread use of 'learning about religion' and 'learning from religion' arose from this approach, and implies that there is an intention to support the pupil in reflecting upon and critically evaluating their own views in the light of their learning about religion and belief.

Today the pendulum seems to be swinging back towards Religious Studies and the systematic study of religions and religion, including the study of non-religious worldviews. However, the ideas and resources in this Teacher's Guide argue that you can have a rigorous study of religion and belief that still gives opportunities for pupils to reflect upon and develop their own ways of thinking in the light of their studies.

On the following pages is an introduction to six approaches or pedagogies that focus on 'informational' and 'formational' approaches to Religious Education, separately and in combination.

Approaching world religions and non-religious worldviews

Many agreed syllabuses use themes to map out the religions covered in RE. These include general, overarching concept-clusters, such as beliefs, teachings and sources of authority, or questions of meaning, purpose and truth (see Essential knowledge, p.30). Or they may focus on themes, such as celebrations, founders and leaders, symbols and religious expression, beliefs in action, ethics and relationships.

Some argue that these artificial structures distort the individual nature of religions, and it is important to note that there is a difference between lived religions on the ground and textbook religions (and this applies to the 'nutshell guides' we have carefully constructed on the following pages). The reality is that looking at religious traditions is more like looking through a kaleidoscope than at a photograph. Religions tend to be fluid, complex and dynamic internally, as well as in their relationships with other traditions and cultures.

In the classroom, we like to explore within neat boundaries (it is easier!), and it is impossible to do full justice to the diversity of faith and belief in our communities, let alone the world. However, our RE should allow pupils to encounter religions as diverse and living, rather than giving the impression that all Christians or all Muslims or all atheists are the same and agree about everything within their communities. We should try to introduce pupils to the kaleidoscope of faith and belief.

1

The phenomena of religion: developing understanding of the observations we make of religion

For example, a teacher plans to introduce a class to the Muslim religion for the first time, and uses a selection of artefacts from the mosque. Pupils are asked to develop their understanding of what Muslims do and what they say and think about their actions. Pupils make a selection of six artefacts, images and texts to sum up all they have learned about the Muslim faith so far.

A phenomenological approach focuses on studying religions (in this case Islam) through stories, moral behaviour, rituals, beliefs, experiences and community life and the art and architecture of the faith.

Taking it further: explore the ideas of Ninian Smart.

2

Experiential RE: educating the spirit, challenging materialist assumptions

For example, a teacher wants to enable spiritual development through RE so uses stilling, guided story and creative imagination to explore religious and spiritual experiences, questions and beliefs increasingly deeply in the classroom. After a guided story on Pesach, which focuses on Jewish concepts of freedom, tradition and community, the pupils express their own spiritual ideas about concepts like these, connecting their experience to Jewish practice thoughtfully. They reflect on the place of concepts of love, sacrifice, submission or thankfulness, creating sculptures or poems.

An experiential approach uses the idea that children have some spiritual capacities of their own, and develops this through RE by use of creative imagination, in relation to religious materials.

Taking it further: explore the ideas of John Hammond and David Hay.

3

Interpretive RE: the skills of sense-making

For example, starting work on Hindu dharma, a teacher begins with four rather contradictory accounts of how Diwali is practised in local communities and in India today. Emphasising religion as it is lived (not merely history, texts or beliefs), in this approach, pupils become enquirers themselves into the varieties of religion and belief. The key skill of making sense or interpreting gradually extends pupils' awareness of living communities of faith.

Interpretive approaches use authentic accounts of the ways members of religions today practise their faith. These learning methods are aimed at enabling pupils to draw meaning from the encounter with religion for themselves, becoming researchers and enquirers in their lessons.

Taking it further: explore the ideas of Robert Jackson.

Concepts for learning in RE: searching for truth

In the unit about Christian beliefs about God, pupils learn three concepts: Incarnation, Trinity and Salvation. They enquire into the ways these concepts make sense of the Christmas and Easter narratives, and how these concepts illuminate the meanings of the festivals that are celebrated. They develop understanding of beliefs, and think about how beliefs can be tested by argument or experience, moving towards analysing truth claims from religion for themselves.

Conceptual learning, for religious literacy, takes key concepts from religions and worldviews and from Religious Studies as a discipline, and enables pupils to increase their ability to understand and analyse religions and beliefs in relation to ideas of truth.

Taking it further: explore the ideas of Andrew Wright or Trevor Cooling.

Ultimate questions as a focus in RE: using insights from religion in pupils' personal development

Pupils begin a unit of work by raising all the questions they would like to ask of God / the creator / the Supreme Being / the ultimate brain. With stimulus from religious texts and practices, the class use a 'Philosophy for Children' (P4C) method. A 'community of enquiry' activity explores the pupils' own questions: what is the 'ultimate question' for each pupil? Afterwards, the class develop pieces of personal work using their own and religious ideas about the ultimate questions explored and the methods by which answers might be found and evaluated.

A humanising approach uses 'big questions' of meaning, purpose and truth to explore the impact of religion on life, to construct meaning and to challenge the learners to deepen their own ideas.

Taking it further: explore the ideas of Michael Grimmitt.

Pupils' worldviews in RE

To learn about commitment and values, pupils begin with their own commitments, and generalise from these. Exploring the ways their everyday commitments can be structured into a view of what matters, a view of the world, is more important than gathering understanding of religion, as the aim of RE is to clarify the learner's vision of life. Religions are seen not primarily as phenomena or belief systems but as ways of looking at the world. Atheist and spiritual perspectives are as valid as those which come from religion.

A worldviews approach develops pupils' own answers to human questions, using religious ideas and teachings as a challenging resource for pupils' own development of perspective, opinion and point of view.

Taking it further: explore the ideas of Clive Erricker.

There is a range of ways of teaching RE. These pages introduce six pedagogies. More detail can be found in Michael Grimmitt, *Pedagogies of Religious Education* (McCrimmons 2000).

A brief outline of Buddhist belief and practice

Buddhism was founded by Siddhartha Gautama, who lived in India in the sixth century BCE. He was brought up in luxury, but when he encountered suffering he left his palace and spent his life in the search for answers to the questions posed by human suffering, desire and the search for happiness.

After following severe and ascetic practices for some years, he came to realise that punishing the human body in an effort to understand suffering would not yield answers. He developed the Middle Way of growing in wisdom, morality and mindfulness, and built up a large following of disciples.

Siddhartha reached enlightenment at the age of 35 and was given the title 'Buddha', or 'enlightened one'. Some Buddhist teachings say that there were others who attained enlightenment before Gautama Buddha.

Enlightenment is a state of total understanding, peace and compassion. According to Buddhist teaching, the Buddha could have left the cycle of life, death and rebirth when he achieved enlightenment, but stayed with his followers for the remaining 40 years of his life, teaching the way to liberation from suffering.

The Buddha is greatly honoured for his teaching, but is not worshipped as God. There is diversity between Buddhist traditions: most do not pray to Buddha, although some do; some see Buddhism as a religion, whereas others prefer to see it as a philosophy and way of life.

The Three Treasures (Refuges)

Buddhists take refuge in three treasures:

- the **Buddha** (the inspiration of this enlightened being and his teachings)
- the **dhamma** (the teaching of the Buddha)
- the **sangha** (the community of Buddhists)

The Four Noble Truths

These are four tenets that all Buddhists accept:

- Life involves suffering (or 'unsatisfactoriness' – dukkha). It is not difficult to see that there is suffering and unhappiness in life, both in the world at large and within a person.
- The cause of suffering is desire (tanha). People do not like suffering and unhappiness: it is what they want to move away from. To do this, people need to understand and remove its causes.
- It is possible to end suffering (nirodha) by replacing craving and desire with inner satisfaction. The point at which this is achieved is called Nibbana (Nirvana), a state of peace and happiness. This is a goal that all can move towards.
- Following the Eightfold Path (see below) leads to Nibbana (Nirvana) and the cessation of suffering. This is the path of growth and development that enables people to cultivate the positive in all aspects of life. An individual takes responsibility to make progress along this path. There is no external judgement in Buddhism. People move at their own pace, and achieve enlightenment by their own heroic attempts.

The Noble Eightfold Path

This is a practical guide to living within the teachings of the Buddha in every aspect of life.

Steps to wisdom (knowing in a 'Buddha-like' way)	Ethical steps (treating the world and others in a 'Buddha-like' way)	Mental steps (approaching life in a 'Buddha-like' way)
1. Right understanding 2. Right thought	3. Right speech 4. Right action 5. Right livelihood	6. Right effort 7. Right mindfulness 8. Right concentration

The Five Precepts or Principles

The following principles guide most Buddhists' ways of living:

1 To refrain from destroying or harming living beings

2 To refrain from taking that which is not freely given (stealing)

3 To refrain from sexual misconduct (improper sexual behaviour)

4 To refrain from incorrect speech and deceiving

5 To refrain from intoxicants that lead to loss of mindfulness or carelessness.

Buddhist philosophy and practices

Buddhism teaches the law of kamma (karma), where every thought or action sows the seed of a positive or negative nature. This connects with teaching about rebirth.

Meditation is practised throughout Buddhist traditions, although styles vary.

Whilst Buddhist monks and nuns are often highly visible, most Buddhists follow the path as lay people. The community shares the task of alleviating suffering, supports its monks and nuns, recognises and supports its leaders and celebrates such festivals as Wesak, remembering the birth, enlightenment and death of the Buddha.

Many Buddhists do not attend temples, but practise meditation and chanting in shrines in their homes or gardens. Use of shrines, paintings and iconography is common but varied.

Enlightenment

The unifying doctrine of the various Buddhist traditions is the enlightenment experience of the Buddha. Enlightenment is not a place but a state of being, based on wisdom and compassion. It is hard for ordinary humans to comprehend, but is the end result of an attempt to master the truth for oneself. In Buddhist scriptures there are examples of almost-instantaneous enlightenment and of enlightenment taking many lifetimes.

Unless someone gains enlightenment, Buddhism teaches that she or he will continue to be re-born. Most traditions see the goal for a Buddhist to be Nibbana (Nirvana), where one breaks out of the cycle of rebirth. Some traditions emphasise the Bodhisattva principle, whereby an arhat (an enlightened being) puts others before him or herself in order to help and support all sentient beings in all realms. Some Buddhists strive for full Buddhahood.

Schools within Buddhism

There are two main schools within Buddhism:

- Theravada Buddhism, meaning 'teachings of the elders'. This is the dominant form of Buddhism in Thailand and Sri Lanka, for example. Theravadan scriptures are written in Pali. Terms include dhamma, kamma, nibbana and sutta.
- Mahayana Buddhism, meaning 'great vehicle'. Tibetan Buddhism is a part of the Mahayana tradition. Mahayana texts are usually written in Sanskrit, which is why there is different spelling of some key words. Sanskrit terms include dharma, karma, nirvana and sutra.

Buddhist scriptures

Tipitaka (also the Pali Canon), meaning 'three baskets'

These are three types of writings collected by Buddhists as guidance and wisdom after the death of the Buddha. The three baskets comprise:

1 Sutta Pitaka (sutta are collections of the Buddha's sayings and teachings in his lifetime), written originally in Pali, the North Indian language he spoke.

2 Abhidhamma Pitaka: philosophical discussions of the meanings of the Buddha's teaching.

3 Vinaya Pitaka, rules and precepts for Buddhist monastics to live in the way of the Buddha.

These are the texts commonly used within the Theravada tradition.

Mahayana sutras

In addition to the above, Mahayana Buddhists use many other sutras ('threads' or 'rules' in Sanskrit), such as the well-known Lotus Sutra.

There are many texts in Buddhism. The Dhammapada and the Tibetan Book of the Dead are two influential examples.

Buddhism today

From its beginnings in India, many schools and traditions developed within Buddhism. The Buddhist path is very influential in India, China, Japan, Thailand, Tibet, Burma, Sri Lanka and many other countries. Each country has adapted and adopted Buddhism within its culture and traditions, hence there is great diversity within and between Buddhists.

The main forms of Buddhism practised in the UK today are Tibetan, various forms of Theravada (as practised in Thailand and Sri Lanka), Zen (as practised in Japan and Vietnam) and Pure Land (as practised in China). Triratna (formerly Friends of the Western Buddhist Order) was founded in London in 1967 and is now an important part of the wider Buddhist community in the UK and beyond. The Dalai Lama, a leader of Tibetan Buddhism, is a very influential figure. Thich Nhat Hahn is a revered Zen master from Vietnam and proponent of 'Engaged Buddhism'.

Worldwide, there are approximately 488 million Buddhists. In the UK, according to the 2011 UK census, there are around 178,000 Buddhists.

A brief outline of Buddhist belief and practice

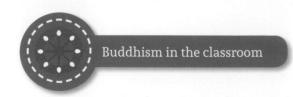

Buddhism in the classroom

Buddhism makes an interesting study because it is the only major religious tradition to have no god. It raises philosophical questions as well as practical ones. It offers a diagnosis of the human condition and then a treatment that differs from those offered by the Abrahamic faith traditions. The close links between Buddhist meditation and the increasingly popular practice of 'mindfulness' meditation are also worth exploring.

A balanced programme of study should include material which aims to develop understanding of:

• the life and teachings of the Buddha

• teaching, doctrines and values both studied in themselves and exemplified through practices

• Buddhists and Buddhism in Britain today.

The suggestions below are designed to help teachers of different age groups to plan active RE work with a focus on Buddhism. They are intended to be used flexibly and as part of active learning (see pp.44–47).

Working with 6–8 year olds

• Re-tell stories. Ask: What happened to the young Siddhartha to make him leave his palace? What was he looking for? Talk about what pupils are looking for in life.

• Explore different images of the Buddha. Ask: Why do they look the way they do? What are they used for? Who values them? Find out about the meaning of the Buddha's hand gestures and the other marks on his body.

• Think about not causing harm. Talk about hurting others, including creatures. Ask: Why does this happen? Could it be stopped?

• Make a 'wheel' or 'stepping stones' pictures to illustrate the Eightfold Path. Give examples of what some of the steps on the path might mean in the playground or in the family.

• Consider the symbols most commonly used for Buddhism – the wheel and the lotus flower. Make links between these symbols and some Buddhist doctrines and actions.

• Think about suffering and happiness for young children. What do they think causes suffering and what do they think leads to happiness? What do they think about the idea that good and bad things do not last?

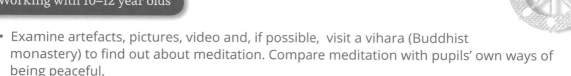

Working with 10–12 year olds

- Examine artefacts, pictures, video and, if possible, visit a vihara (Buddhist monastery) to find out about meditation. Compare meditation with pupils' own ways of being peaceful.
- Create collages of happiness, relating to different ages, origins and so on; use the collages to explore the limits to happiness and its impermanence.
- Talk about the Five Precepts. Ask: Would they make a perfect world? Do the pupils agree with them or practise them? What five precepts would they offer to the world? Do they keep these themselves?
- Think about the opposites to the Eightfold Path and discuss the meaning of each of the Buddhist steps, giving examples of the behaviour that would go with them. Use these opposites to understand the Eightfold Path.
- Connect Buddhist ideas about suffering with the practices of compassion, meditation and vegetarianism.

Working with 14–16 year olds

- Apply the Buddha's 'prescription' for the ending of suffering to examples of modern social or personal problems. Evaluate how effectively they might work. Find out about Western Buddhists who believe they do.
- Read and explore some stories or wise sayings from the Pali Canon, e.g. a dramatic story in Majjhima Nikaya 86 (the second book of the Sutta Pitaka) where the Buddha stands up to Angulimala, a robber and murderer, who then becomes a disciple. Explain what the Buddha is saying about wisdom, justice and strength in this story. Analyse ways in which 'engaged Buddhism' promotes peace and justice.
- Explore diverse perspectives on Buddhism in British Buddhist communities. Compare the outlooks of a traditional perspective (e.g. Tibetan or Pure Land) with a recent perspective (e.g. Triratna). Find out what it means to be Buddhist in a British context.
- Explore Buddhist ethics as practised in the UK, for example, in prison chaplaincy or work with drug addicts.
- Discuss what it means to be a Buddhist and an atheist.
- Compare Buddhist ethics with Humanist ethics. Is Buddhism an early form of Humanism?
- Investigate what it is about Buddhism that makes it attractive to Westerners. Analyse how it is marketed and used in marketing. Evaluate whether its interpretation as a philosophy makes it 'acceptable' to a secular media or society.

A brief outline of Christian belief and practice

Christianity began in the first century CE as a radical element within Judaism. It is rooted in the life and teaching of Jesus of Nazareth, a first-century Jew from Galilee.

The early Jesus movements were linked strongly to Jewish life, but as the tradition spread it came to include Gentiles (those of non-Jewish background). With the conversion of the Roman Emperor Constantine in the early fourth century CE, Christianity became the official religion of the Roman Empire and spread rapidly throughout the world.

The essence (or core) of Christian belief is expressed in several creeds. There are three main creeds:

1 the Apostles' Creed*

2 the Nicene Creed*

3 the Athanasian Creed

* the most commonly used and important

The creeds express belief in the Trinity: that God is three persons in one – Father (Creator), Jesus (the Son and Saviour) and the Holy Spirit (Sustainer and Comforter).

The Apostles' Creed

I believe in God, the Father almighty,
creator of heaven and earth.
I believe in Jesus Christ, God's only Son, our Lord,
who was conceived by the Holy Spirit,
born of the Virgin Mary,
suffered under Pontius Pilate,
was crucified, died and was buried;
he descended to the dead.
On the third day he rose again;
he ascended into heaven,
he is seated at the right hand of the Father,
and he will come to judge the living and the dead.
I believe in the Holy Spirit,
the holy catholic Church,
the communion of saints,
the forgiveness of sins,
the resurrection of the body,
and the life everlasting.

Amen

Jesus

The person of Jesus is central to all Christian belief and worship. Jesus is both a historical figure and a person of religious significance, being seen as Saviour and Lord, and God incarnate (i.e. 'in the flesh').

Key features in Jesus' life:

- birth and childhood
- baptism and temptations
- call of disciples and continuing relationship with them
- teaching through parables, miracles, the Beatitudes and the Great Commandment or Golden Rule
- Holy Week (Palm Sunday to burial)
- resurrection, ascension and second coming.

Jesus and his teachings are expressed through:

- lives of Christians through the ages and today
- worship, festivals, rituals and celebrations
- how Jesus is portrayed in the arts
- how belief in Jesus has influenced cultures and ways of life.

The Bible

The Bible is a collection of 66 books. The canon (list) of books chosen for inclusion was decided in 397 CE. There are two sections:

 The Old Testament (39 books) was written over a period of some 1000 years and includes laws, myths, poetry, songs, prophecies, history, narratives and stories.

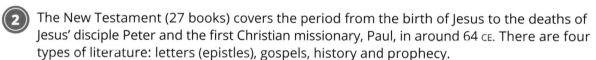 The New Testament (27 books) covers the period from the birth of Jesus to the deaths of Jesus' disciple Peter and the first Christian missionary, Paul, in around 64 CE. There are four types of literature: letters (epistles), gospels, history and prophecy.

All Christians refer to the Bible and regard it as a source of authority, but within different traditions or denominations there is a variety of ways in which it is read, understood and followed.

The Apocrypha (15 writings) was composed between 300 BCE and 100 CE. This collection contains lengthy books, short letters and extracts. These writings may be included with the Old Testament, or printed as a separate section between the Old and New Testaments. Not all Christians see it as having the same authority as the other 66 books.

The 'Big Story' of the Bible

Most Christians see the Bible as more than a collection of books: they see it as revealing the relationship between God and God's people. The story can be summed up in some of the big concepts in Christianity.

- **Creation** – God created a good world and humans are important in it.
- **Fall** – humans rebel against God and sin; this ruptures the relationship between humans and God.
- **Covenant** – God sets up an agreement (covenant) with the Hebrew (Jewish) people to begin to repair the damage and bring humans back to a relationship with God.
- **Exile** – the people of God keep failing their side of the bargain; eventually the people are taken into exile. The plan seems to have failed.
- **Messiah** – the people of God look to God to send a Rescuer, a Saviour, a 'Chosen' or 'Anointed One' (Messiah or Christ).

- **Incarnation** – the plan is rebooted by the sending of Jesus, God incarnate (in the flesh). Christians see Jesus as the Messiah.
- **Gospel** – Jesus brings the 'good news' that, through him, sin can be overcome and the relationship with God can be healed.
- **Salvation** – Jesus' willing sacrifice breaks the power of sin in people's lives and opens up the path to God.
- **Kingdom of God** – the rule of God has begun in the world wherever Christians love God and love their neighbour.
- **Heaven** – this life is not the end; it is a preparation for eternal life with God in a new, restored creation.

Not all Christians agree with this version of the 'big story', but it helps to make sense of the importance and role of Jesus, for example.

Denominations within Christianity

Over the course of history Christianity has broken up into a number of different churches or denominations. There are three broad groups.

- **The Orthodox Church** is mainly found in Eastern Europe, Russia and the Eastern Mediterranean.
- **The Roman Catholic Church** is found in all parts of the world, accounting for some 60 per cent of all Christians.
- **The Protestant churches** were established as a result of the sixteenth-century Reformation and include the Church of England (the Anglican Church, and the world Anglican Communion), Baptists, Methodists, the Salvation Army, Pentecostals, Quakers and Presbyterians.

The Christian year

The Christian year begins with the first Sunday of Advent (the fourth Sunday before 25 December). The Church has set out a cycle by which all the main events in the life of Jesus and the saints are remembered and reflected upon.

The most important festivals for Christians are Easter, Pentecost and Christmas. While the details of how Christians around the world celebrate these festivals may vary considerably, there are likely to be some common features:

- reading of and reflection on the festival story
- special services and acts of devotion
- symbols and artefacts
- social events within the church community.

Christianity today

Christianity was introduced into Britain from continental Europe in the early years of the Common Era (CE), and is the largest and longest established of the world religions in the country. The Christian tradition in the UK is ethnically and denominationally diverse, developing as immigrants brought with them their own distinctive traditions and expressions of faith.

Worldwide, there are approximately 2.18 billion Christians. In Britain, approximately 33.2 million identified themselves as Christian on the 2011 census.

 Christianity in the classroom

It is important for pupils to recognise that there is great diversity within Christianity. Even within a single denomination there will be differences in the interpretation and application of the Bible, for example.

A balanced programme of study should include material which aims to develop understanding of:

- Jesus as a historical person and focus of faith as Saviour and Lord
- Christianity as a diverse world religion
- teaching, beliefs, stories/texts and values
- festivals, rituals and practices.

The suggestions below are designed to help, teachers with different age groups to plan active RE work with a focus on Christianity.

Teaching methods need to be varied and stimulating, and make use of active learning strategies (see pp.44–47).

 Working with 6–8 year olds

- Talk about Jesus teaching his followers by using stories. Read some of Jesus' parables. Use dance and drama to explore the meanings of Jesus' parables. Ask: What is the 'good news' Jesus brings?
- Visit a church; talk with the vicar, minister or priest. Explore the symbolism of artefacts. Ask: What does the Church show is most important to Christians? Create class guides to the local church. Ask some Christians: 'What is so important about Jesus?' Learn the meaning of 'Incarnation' – Jesus as God in the flesh.
- Find out about the Bible. Ask: How did the Bible come into being? How is the Bible understood and used by Christians in different times and places?
- Explore a Christian festival or ceremony. Ask: What happens, when and why? Talk about feelings when people celebrate like this.
- Talk about the importance of baptism for Christians. Ask: What is involved in belonging to a religion?

Working with 10–12 year olds

- Explore how Christians interpret different texts in the Bible, for example, Genesis 1. Find out why some Christians become scientists.

- Read about Jesus performing miracles. Ask: What do the miracles of Jesus mean? Examine and debate the question of whether God performs miracles now, interviewing witnesses for both sides of the argument.

- Explore what it means to be a Christian in Britain today. Find out how Christians put Jesus' teaching and example into practice. Ask: Does it take guts to stand up for being a Christian in the world?

- Recognise and interpret key symbols in Christian art, worship and language. Ask: How have Christians expressed their beliefs through the creative and expressive arts?

- Compare Christian places of worship. Ask: What is their significance in the lives of believers? How do places of worship reveal similarities and differences between Christians? If God is everywhere, why do people need to worship in church?

- Explore the multicultural nature of Christianity, and its various denominations and traditions. Ask: How is this diversity reflected in the community where pupils live? How do people with different beliefs get on?

Working with 14–16 year olds

- Outline a Christian understanding of the 'salvation narrative' of the Bible. Explain the theological significance to Christians of Jesus' life, death and resurrection.

- Explain different ways in which Christians interpret texts, such as Genesis 1, the resurrection narratives and the book of Revelation. Account for the different impact of these interpretations.

- Debate the extent of the impact of Jesus Christ on history, and on the current structure of Western society. To what extent has this impact been positive?

- Explore the concept of 'church' as outlined by Paul. Discuss how 'church' today is understood and experienced within different denominations or traditions.

- Interview some practising Christians. Identify and write about the ways in which faith affects the way Christians live their lives today.

- Discuss and evaluate the extent to which contemporary culture in the UK is affecting the practice of Christianity. What are the implications for values in the lives of individual Christians? And for pupils of different beliefs?

- Research liberation theology and evaluate how far this approach to Christianity fits the character and teaching of Jesus. Was Jesus a liberation theologian?

- Identify the Bible passages which refer to the Christian belief in life after death. Reflect on pupils' own beliefs. Account for different beliefs and their impact on how people live.

A brief outline of Hindu belief and practice

The world religion known as 'Hinduism' is generally regarded as the world's oldest, with its roots in the Indus Valley civilisation, probably in the 4th–2nd centuries BCE. It consists of multiple spiritual and practical paths. The word 'Hindu' comes from the Sanskrit word 'Sindh' after the River Sindh (Indus in English), which flows through India and Pakistan, and the civilisation that grew up along it.

Hinduism is often called Dharma or the Sanatana Dharma (eternal way) by those who practise it.

The Hindu tradition is ancient in origin, diverse, inclusive and ever-changing. It may help in understanding the Hindu way to think of it as many streams merging into a huge river, flowing into a delta, with many waterways leading into the sea, or a giant banyan tree with many roots and branches but one trunk.

As in other religions, diversity plays a major part within Hinduism. Therefore, beliefs and practices vary according to historical streams, geographical locations and cultural traditions. Similarly, there is a wide range of schools of thought, philosophical positions, religious practices and foci for devotion that are accepted.

For some, it is their *cultural identity* that matters, for others their *heritage* and for others it's the *spirituality* of the faith that matters. This means that there are many ways to be a Hindu. To follow Sanatana Dharma is really to find one's own path to the Divine: all rituals, customs and 'rules' are only a possible way to be a Hindu, not *the* way – there is no one way. Within this diversity, however, there are some beliefs and practices that are more universally accepted, for example the authority of sacred texts called the Vedas (meaning 'knowledge' in Sanskrit).

The Hindu way

The Hindu way has four aims (punusharthas):

- **dharma:** religious or moral duty
- **artha:** economic development, providing for family and society by honest means
- **kama:** regulated enjoyment of the pleasures and beauty of life
- **moksha:** liberation from the cycle of birth and rebirth; reincarnation.

A Hindu is true to his or her dharma if all appropriate religious and moral duties are carried out.

Hindu beliefs

Dharma

The key concept of dharma frames a Hindu's life. It describes Hindu social and moral duty. Hindus aim to live in conformity with their dharma, and aiming to maintain this will inform all or many aspects of their life. Dharma varies according to the personal path individual Hindus have taken and the circumstances of life.

Brahman

Brahman represents the concept of God in Hinduism. Brahman is seen as the source of all life, the sum total of all souls in the universe, present in every living thing and the 'place' or state of being that is moksha. Brahman is too infinite to be understood by the human intellect, but humans can come to Brahman, the Ultimate, through the many Hindu deities – gods and goddesses – all of whom represent an aspect of Brahman's character or being. Other deities through whom Brahman is worshipped are Lord Vishnu, Lord Shiva, Lord Ganesh (or 'Ganpati'), Goddess Lakshmi, Goddess Parvati, Goddess Sarasvati and Durga Mata.

Atman

The atman refers to the 'eternal self' or 'soul', the 'essence' of a single being. When the body dies, the atman moves into a new body in the process known as samsara, or reincarnation. Hindus believe Brahman is present in the atman, which is in all living things, and the elements – earth, air, fire and water.

Karma

The atman returns to the earth in another body according to the law of karma. This translates as 'action' or 'deed', but its wider meaning is 'cause and effect'. Karma refers to the sum of a Hindu's actions, which will determine his or her future existences. A life lived in accordance with one's dharma means future reincarnation in a body with more potential to reach Brahman/moksha.

Samsara

Samsara describes the cycle of birth, death and rebirth (reincarnation). The life one is born into depends on how the previous life has been lived, or how far the individual kept or performed his or her dharma. There is no personal judgement of the individual. Together, the laws of karma and samsara provide cosmic, but impersonal, balance.

Moksha

Moksha describes the ultimate goal of all Hindus: liberation from the cycle of samsara and the constant pain of rebirth. There are different ways to attain moksha and one path says that by following one's dharma, one slowly achieves more and more favourable births. Moksha is sometimes described as a drop of water meeting the ocean, as the atman is finally reunited with Brahman.

Community, traditions and worship

The family community is an important focus for faith among many Hindus. Respect for older members of the family, the tradition of marking stages of life by rituals – samskaras – and progressing in devotion or faith towards renunciation of earthly life, all combine to enrich Hindu community life. Hindu community and social life involves a sense of belonging to a wider family as well as (for many Hindus, especially in India) to a varna and caste, or jati, the traditional systems of occupations and social classes.

It is in the family that the long tradition of worship, community and values is most often shared with each generation, made alive in practice, and drawn upon for strength, security, peace and purpose.

Sacred texts

Hindu faith is rooted in scriptures. A number of Hindu sacred texts each have an important place.

Vedas

These are the oldest Hindu texts, emerging from the ancient oral tradition of India, and reaching their present form around 1200–200 BCE. For hundreds, maybe thousands, of years the Vedas were passed on orally before they were written down. They contain hymns of praise to Brahman, rituals, prayers, worship and meditation instructions as well as meditations on the nature of Brahman. The last set of books, called the Upanishads, explores Hindu philosophy. The philosophy and theology in the Upanishads was shared and discussed in an oral tradition lasting into the sixteenth century.

Mahabharata

Composed between 500 and 200 BCE, this text recounts stories of a powerful family, the Bharata, combined with theological discussion. The Mahabharata contains the world's longest poem, the Bhagavad Gita, a dialogue between the royal warrior Arjuna and his charioteer Krishna, exploring dharma, the atman/soul and the nature of God.

Ramayana

This well-loved story was composed in the same period as the Mahabharata. It tells the tale of Prince Rama whose wife, Princess Sita, was abducted by the demon Ravana and was helped by the monkey god Hanuman. This tale, which is remembered at the festival of Diwali, is considered to be about the triumph of good over evil and the importance of dharma.

Hinduism today

The origins of the Sanatana Dharma are in ancient India, yet its contemporary expressions are to be found all over the world, in Africa, the Caribbean and Europe as well as in Asia.

Worldwide, there are approximately 1 billion Hindus. In the UK, according to the 2011 census, there are around 817,000 Hindus (1.5 per cent of the population).

Hinduism in the classroom

Hindu religious traditions are accessible for pupils of all ages. Over the centuries vibrant and fascinating artistic representations of the major Hindu concepts have developed, which are a great 'way in' for pupils to explore Hinduism.

A balanced programme of study should include opportunities for pupils to think about:

- practices such as worship, festivals, pilgrimage, etc.
- theology/major Hindu concepts
- sacred texts
- differences in Hindu traditions
- modern Hindu community and family life.

The suggestions below are designed to help teachers with different age groups to plan active RE work with a focus on Hinduism. They are intended to be used flexibly and as part of active learning (see p.44–47).

Working with 6–8 year olds

- Listen to stories about Hindu gods, goddesses and heroes. Look at some images of the gods and goddesses. Recognise some of the symbols used in these and make links to the stories.
- Watch and recreate dramatic retellings of Hindu epic stories through drama, puppets or dance.
- Find out about Hindu children in Britain, their lives and traditions. What similarities and differences are there with the lives of children who are not Hindus or from a Hindu background?
- Listen to and talk about wise Hindu sayings about the value of animals, plants and the natural world, as well as other people. Explore how these might apply to the modern world.
- Practise greetings (e.g. Hello, Bonjour, Namaste, Peace be with you) and associated hand gestures. Learn that the Hindu greeting 'Namaste' means 'the divine spark in me greets the spark of God in you'. Talk about what difference this makes to a Hindu.
- Use artefacts to see how all five senses are in used in Hindu worship.

Working with 10–12 year olds

- Use images as 'windows' into Hindu ideas about life. 'Wow' students with incredible images of Hindu life, such as the festival of Holi, the burning ghats at Varanasi or sadhus (ascetics) meditating at a mountain shrine, to lead them into the exploration of Hindu theology.
- Visit a Hindu mandir. There are an increasing number in Britain, many with their own education programmes. Find out how worship in the mandir uses the five senses.
- Use Hindu artefacts such as murtis (images and statues) of the gods and goddesses and the puja (worship) tray and, along with sacred texts, explore symbols of the powers and attributes of the divine.
- Make pictorial charts of the life cycle and think about both the rituals and the beliefs associated with our passing lives. Infer wider ethical and social implications from these stages, such as sannyasa – renouncing worldly possessions to focus on Brahman.
- Learn about key Hindu ideas of Brahman, atman, dharma, karma, samsara and moksha. Devise diagrams to show how these ideas fit together. Find out how 'snakes and ladders' (based on the moksha chitram game) reflects Hindu ideas about karma and samsara.

Working with 14–16 year olds

- Explore British Hindu teenagers' lives, their multiple identities and thoughts about their traditions. Investigate what they think about goals in life, connecting with dharma, artha, karma and moksha. Compare similarities and differences with the diverse lives of pupils in your class.
- Explore Hindu commitments to non-violence (ahimsa), harmlessness and vegetarian food. Contrast this with some Western attitudes. Evaluate the proposition that the Hindu path is our best hope in the battle to protect the environment.
- Deepen understanding of atman, Brahman, karma, samsara. Examine what this means for understanding of the self, God and all other living things.
- Analyse sacred texts dealing with dharma, such as passages from the Bhagavad Gita or the Ramayana. Explore the idea of dharma and varna in modern Indian and British Hindu communities. Evaluate this system of social organisation.
- Investigate the way religious beliefs and social traditions are explored/portrayed in Bollywood films.
- Compare British Hindu views towards traditional norms such as varna or the roles of women with traditional and modern Indian views. Consider the contrast in how some Hindus view women and worship of goddesses. Articulate possible causes of this contrast.

Judaism was the world's first monotheistic faith, dating back to Abraham's radical break with the polytheism of the ancient Middle East in around 1900 BCE. Abraham was called into a covenant with God. In return for obedience and loyalty, he was promised a people numbering as many as the dust of the earth and the stars in the sky, the people who became the Jews. Jewish people believe in one God, the creator, beyond space and time, yet a personal God, interested in humanity, and intimately involved with the world, caring for and loving creation. In general, Jewish people do not talk about beliefs – there is no Jewish creed; instead, Judaism is very much about daily practice and religious observance.

Some areas of fundamental importance in Judaism are:

- **God**
- the **Torah**
- the **people and the land**

God

Jews believe in one creator God who cares for all people. Jews worship God, saying blessings and thanks, and believe that they are the chosen people.

Many Jewish people avoid saying and writing God's name, and so in a Jewish context, it might be printed as 'G-d'.

The Jewish prayer the Shema begins with words that are a fundamental expression of Jewish belief: 'Hear, O Israel: The LORD our God is one LORD; and you shall love the LORD your God with all your heart, and with all your soul, and with all your might' (Deuteronomy 6:4–5).

Parts of the Shema are written on a mezuzah (parchment on which religious text is written, which is generally placed inside a small decorative box) and attached to the doorposts of Jewish homes, to be remembered each time it is passed. Parts of the Shema are also placed inside tefillin, the prayer boxes worn on the head and left arm of many Jews, especially Orthodox and Conservative, when they pray.

The Torah

The Torah, meaning teaching, instruction or law, is the main Jewish holy book. The term is used in a wider sense to mean the first five books of the Hebrew Bible (the same in content as the Old Testament of the Christian Bible) and the Talmud – oral law or 'Oral Torah' explaining the Torah. The Torah contains the Ten Commandments given to Moses and the 613 mitzvot or the Jewish laws/commandments (halakha) that observant Jews obey. It also focuses on the Jews' relationship with God and contains songs, prayers and wise sayings.

The whole Hebrew Bible includes:

- the TeNaKh, 'written Torah', which consists of the Torah (law; the first five books), Nevi'im (Prophets) and the Ketuvim (Writings)
- the Talmud, or oral law, which is made up of the Mishnah (the first writing down of this oral law in about 200 CE) and the Gemara (a commentary on the Mishnah).

The Torah is held in great esteem and kept in a special place in the synagogue called the Ark. A weekly portion is read aloud in the Shabbat synagogue service and there is an annual cycle of readings, culminating in the festival of Simchat Torah ('rejoicing in the Torah'). Torah scrolls are taken from the Ark and carried or danced around the synagogue seven times.

Many Jews regularly study the Torah – to do so is to worship God.

The people and the land

The family and home are very important in Jewish life. Shabbat, or the Jewish day of rest, starts at sunset on Friday and lasts until three stars appear in the sky on Saturday. Friday nights are special, involving time at the synagogue, prayers, a meal with family and friends and the chance to rest, discuss and focus on God. Whilst Jewish practice of Shabbat may vary across the different traditions, the coming together of families every weekend, and the wider community for Shabbat services, has been at the heart of Jewish community life for centuries. The instructions in the Shema to 'teach these laws thoroughly to your children, speak of them when you sit in your house' are obeyed as part of Shabbat. Shabbat celebrates the seventh day of creation – the day of rest – and is called 'the day of delight' in some Jewish traditions. Refraining from work is seen by many as a release from the pressure of modern life rather than a restriction.

Kashrut is the body of Jewish law dealing with the foods that are fit to be eaten. These laws, found in the Torah, have existed for more than 3000 years and continue to play an important part in the daily lives of many observant Jews. Food that meets the demands of kashrut is called kosher (fit). 'Keeping kosher' involves eating only certain animals that have been killed in a special way, and using separate sets of kitchen utensils for milk and meat products, which must not be mixed. Food that is forbidden is trefah or treyf ('torn').

The land of Israel is at the heart of Jewish identity for Jews all over the world. Israel is the land promised to Abraham and his descendants by God, where Jews lived for hundreds of years, and is the site of the last remaining wall of the Jewish Temple today. In 70 CE Roman invaders largely destroyed the Temple and threw the Jewish people out of their homeland. They remained exiled until the State of Israel was declared in 1948, following the Second World War and the Nazi Holocaust. During the centuries of Jewish exile various settlers, including many Muslims, came to live in the area around Jerusalem, Palestine. The land is now an area of far-from-resolved conflict between Israel and Palestine.

Judaism today

Worldwide, there are approximately 14 million Jewish people. In the UK, according to the 2011 census, there are around 263,000 Jewish people (0.5 per cent of the population). Jewish people have long been associated with the UK, with the first Jewish settlers coming after the Norman Conquest in 1066. The UK Jewish population consists of both Sephardi (originally from Spain, Portugal and the Middle East) and Ashkenazi Jews (of central and east European origin), with Ashkenazi Jews being the larger group. Within British Judaism, there are two main movements: Orthodox and Progressive. Both believe in the importance of the Torah, but they place different emphasis on it.

Orthodox Jews

Orthodox Jews believe that both the Torah and the oral law contained in the Talmud have been revealed by God and as such contain God's unchanging words. For example, the Torah specifies no 'work' may be undertaken on Shabbat. 'Work' is closely defined in the Mishnah (the written version of the Oral Torah) to include 39 types of activities. This underpins modern Orthodox Jewish practice not to answer the phone, turn on a light or drive on Shabbat.

Hasidic Jews

Hasidic (from the word *chesed*, meaning 'loving kindness' or 'piety') Judaism originally developed as a form of mysticism, bringing God and the Torah into every aspect of ordinary life and is one movement within ultra-Orthodox Judaism.

Progressive Jews

Progressive Jews (sometimes called Liberal or Reform Jews) believe that the Torah was inspired by God, but written down by humans according to God's will. Therefore they may believe that God's law can be reinterpreted, and the laws brought up to date for today.

Conservative Jews

Conservative Jews have developed and emerged as a group somewhere between Orthodox and Progressive Judaism. Masorti is the name given to Conservative Judaism in the UK, Israel and other countries outside of the US and Canada (Masorti is Hebrew for 'traditional'). Conservative Jews aim to comply with as much of the Torah as is practicable in modern society, but may compromise in certain respects. For example, some Conservative Jews may drive to synagogue on Shabbat if they would be otherwise unable to join in with public worship.

Secular Jews

Secular Jews are those who identify themselves as Jewish by culture or heritage rather than through religious observance. As with all of the traditions above, there is diversity among secular Jews too.

 Judaism in the classroom

Judaism is a fascinating and ancient religion in which lie the roots of Christian and Islamic theology. However, it is important to study Judaism itself and to do full justice to Judaism as a living faith in its own right. Judaism's rich sources of wisdom, its ancient traditions, food, festivals and epic stories mean it can be accessed and enjoyed by pupils of all ages.

The suggestions below are designed to help teachers with different age groups to plan active RE work with a focus on Judaism. Teaching methods need to be varied and stimulating and make use of active learning strategies (see pp.44–47).

 Working with 6–8 year olds

- Lay a Friday night Shabbat table. Ask: What is the significance of each of the artefacts used? Think about the value of a day of rest. How might it be a 'day of delight'?

- Read and enact the story behind the festival of Purim or Hanukkah. Ask: What do the stories reveal about the nature of God? Talk about what Jewish people might learn from the stories and the celebrations.

- Talk about the words and meaning of the Ten Commandments for the Jewish people in the time of Moses. Work out what must they have been doing if they had to be given these commands. Ask: Do people still act like this today? Talk about why Jewish people (and Christians) still think the Ten Commandments are important today. Act out how they think people should behave towards others and God, based on these commandments.

- Write out the Shema with total concentration, as a religious scribe would. Talk about why a scribe would take so much care over this. Learn about the important meanings in the Shema: the oneness of God and the Jews as the chosen people of God.

- Explore how Jews bring the Shema into their lives: in tefillin and mezuzot. Compare this way of remembering important things with the way pupils remember. Ask: What might make people good 'rememberers'?

Working with 10–12 year olds

- Learn about food that is kosher or trefah. Consider what this ancient system of classification means. Ask why many modern Jews still adhere to it.

- Compare worship traditions and rites of passage across two different Jewish groups, e.g. Orthodox and Progressive. Outline each group's reasons for their way of upholding the traditions.

- Read different textual traditions from the Jewish scriptures, for example the psalms of David and instructions for living found in the book of Deuteronomy. Understand the different purposes of these types of text.

- Learn about the epic story of the Exodus through text, film, art and drama. Explore how this dramatic story is remembered today in the festival of Passover. Find out what it means to Jewish people today.

- Learn a brief history of Israel. Consider the religious and historical factors that make Israel so important to Jews.

 Working with 14–16 year olds

- Compare the ideas about God presented by Exodus and by the scholar Maimonides. Consider how such contrasting ideas about God might be helpful. Get pupils to reflect on their own ideas and questions about God.

- Compare the practices of Orthodox and Progressive Judaism. Discuss: How important are change, continuity and growth within the history of Judaism?

- Learn Jewish theological responses to the Shoah (Holocaust). Analyse the idea that 'theodicy is impossible after Auschwitz'. Articulate what actions we should take to prevent any similar event from ever being possible again. Challenge pupils – are they active in fighting prejudice?

- Consider the part the concept of nationhood has played in the life of the Jewish community. Debate: How far is it possible to separate religion from nationality? Evaluate the arguments.

- Analyse the book of Job. What does this book tell Jewish people about suffering and free will? Compare with the exploration of suffering and free will in Genesis 3. Evaluate the vision of humans and free will in these books. Ask pupils to articulate different perspectives, and justify their own in the light of their learning.

- Learn about the monarchy period as recounted in Samuel and Kings. Explore the theology of leadership within these texts. Relate to theological arguments made by Israel's modern leaders.

A brief outline of Muslim belief and practice

The religion of Islam was revealed to the Prophet Muhammad in the seventh century CE. The word 'Islam' means 'submission' or 'surrender'; the life of a Muslim is spent, therefore, in willing submission to Allah (Arabic for God).

Muhammad

Muhammad (570–632 CE) was born in the Arabian city of Makkah (Mecca) where, from the age of 40, he received a series of revelations from Allah. The revelations were received over a period of 23 years and were delivered by the Angel Jibril (Gabriel). These revelations form Al-Qur'an (the Book), the sacred text of Islam.

Muslims do not believe that Muhammad brought a new faith. Rather, he is seen as the last of a long line of prophets sent by God to guide people on to the right path. Jesus (Isa) was one such prophet. Muhammad is regarded by Muslims as the 'seal of the prophets'. Muslims often follow the Prophet's name with the words 'peace be upon him' (pbuh) as a mark of respect.

Those who accepted Muhammad as the 'seal of the prophets' and his revelations as being from Allah were welcomed into the Muslim community (ummah). This community migrated from Makkah to Madinah (Medina) in 622 CE (the hijrah, or migration), a formative event in the history of Islam.

The Muslim way

Muslims regard Islam as a complete way of life (din, pronounced 'deen'). There are four main concepts within Islam that underpin all Muslim belief and behaviour:

- **tawhid**
- **iman**
- **ibadah**
- **akhlaq**

Tawhid

Tawhid is the oneness of Allah. Islam teaches an absolute monotheism. To regard anyone or anything as being equal to Allah, or even a partner with Allah, is described as *shirk* and is absolutely forbidden. The Muslim confession of faith, the Shahadah, declares: 'There is no god except Allah.' This is not just an abstract theological statement but one that is worked out in many ways. Allah cannot be represented in art, so the geometrical designs so prominent in Islamic culture are a reflection of the unity and beauty of Allah. Using the 99 Names of Allah is helpful in exploring the nature of Allah in Islam.

Iman

Iman is faith, the believer's response to God. Faith is expressed primarily in acceptance of Muhammad as the final messenger of God (in the words of the Shahadah, 'There is no god except Allah; Muhammad is the messenger of Allah') and of Al-Qur'an as the revealed word of God. 'Qur'an' means 'reciting' and is the definitive guide for all Muslims. In Shi'a Islam there are five roots of religion which are similar to Sunni beliefs and include the oneness of God, the Prophets and life after death as well as two areas that are emphasised in the Shi'a tradition. These are the belief that God appointed a series of spiritual guides or imams to guide humankind after the death of the Prophet Muhammad and the belief that God is just and fair.

Ibadah

Muslims use this single word for both worship and any action that is performed with the intention of obeying Allah. Thus worship and belief-in-action are inextricably linked by language. This concept includes the five pillars of Islam, which help Muslims to ensure that their lives are dedicated to the worship of Allah. As the whole of life is worship, no special emphasis is placed on any one aspect of obligation.

The five pillars

The compulsory five pillars provide a structure for the daily spiritual life of the Muslim. All Muslims agree on the importance of these five although Shi'a Muslims may not refer to them by the same names and regard some additional acts as obligatory.

1. Shahadah is the declaration of faith: 'There is no god except Allah; Muhammad is the messenger of Allah.'
2. Salat is ritual prayer carried out five times a day.
3. Zakat is an annual gift for charity, usually 2.5 per cent of income.
4. Sawm is fasting from food and water during the daylight hours of the month of Ramadan.
5. Hajj is pilgrimage to Makkah, to be made at least once in a lifetime if possible.

Akhlaq

Akhlaq is a term that cannot be translated by a single English equivalent. It means behaviour, morality, manners, attitudes, and the social ethical codes by which Muslims should live. Included are aspects of family and social life and also issues for the whole of humanity, e.g. the possibility of an Islamic social and economic order, which is a viable alternative to both capitalism and communism.

Other important Islamic concepts

Ihsan

Some Muslims, especially Sufi Muslims, also emphasise the term ihsan, or excellence/perfection; the term can be translated 'doing what is good, excellent or beautiful'. It refers to right actions, charity, sincerity and goodness. This is outlined in the Hadith of Gabriel (Sahih Bukhari Volume 1, Book 2, Number 47).

Jihad

The Arabic word jihad basically means to struggle, to exert oneself and to strive. Two forms of jihad exist: the 'greater' jihad and the 'lesser' jihad. The greater jihad contains within its meaning the idea of emptying out the spiritual diseases or blameworthy traits of the heart such as anger, jealousy, envy, ignorance and arrogance, etc. and replacing these with praiseworthy traits such as kindness, generosity, mercy, respectfulness and tolerance.

The 'lesser' jihad is struggle against oppression. This does not mean that it is only the act of fighting the enemy. Warfare is the absolute last resort in a 'lesser' jihad and many preconditions have to be met in order to declare it. War can also only be waged if nothing else has been successful. A well-known saying of the Prophet Muhammad on returning from a battle is 'We return from the lesser jihad to the greater jihad.'

Schools within Islam

There are two main schools within Islam.

Sunni Muslims

Sunni Muslims (from the Arabic sunna, meaning 'tradition' or 'example', i.e. the customary practice of the Prophet Muhammad) believe that Abu Bakr, Umar, Uthman and Ali were the rightful successors to Muhammad after the Prophet's death. They believe authority ends with Al-Qur'an and Muhammad, and so, to make decisions on how to live (for example, on whether organ transplants are permitted), the community would consult with those who are knowledgeable about Al-Qur'an, Hadith (the sayings, teachings and deeds of Muhammad) and Sharia, and make a majority decision. Around 80 per cent of Muslims are Sunnis.

Shi'a Muslims

Shi'a Muslims maintain that the rightful leadership of Islam should have passed from Muhammad to Ali (the cousin and son-in-law of Muhammad). Shi'a is an abbreviation of Shi'at Ali, which means 'the party of Ali'. The majority of Shi'a Muslims (or 'Twelvers') believe that Ali and the eleven imams that followed him had special authority to interpret Al-Qur'an and make laws (Sharia). Shi'a Muslims believe that, since Allah was guiding them, the twelve imams had no faults and made no mistakes. Today, most Shi'a Muslims would follow a single scholar, called a marja, or Grand Ayatollah, one of around 60 such maraji in the world. Most British Shi'a Muslims follow Grand Ayatollah Ali Husayni Sistani. Shi'a Muslims live mainly in Iraq, Lebanon, Iran and India.

Islam today

From its origins in Arabia, Islam has spread to Europe (e.g. there has been a significant Muslim influence in Spain for centuries), the Indian subcontinent, Africa, Malaysia and Indonesia.

Muslims have lived in the UK mainly since the early nineteenth century. The largest Muslim communities are found in the West Midlands, Lancashire, West Yorkshire, Greater London and central Scotland. Most major towns and cities have a sizeable Muslim population.

Worldwide, there are approximately 1.62 billion Muslims. In the UK, according to the 2011 census, there are around 2.8 million Muslims (4.4 per cent of the population).

Islam in the classroom

It is appropriate for pupils of any school age to study Islam. Many syllabuses require this, and others make it optional. It is important to recognise that there is no single 'Islam', and that there is a real diversity in Muslim practice in the UK and worldwide, so that there are different expressions of practice that can be equally valid.

A balanced programme of study should include material which aims to develop understanding of:

• Prophet Muhammad
• teaching, beliefs and values
• sources of authority: Al-Qur'an and Hadith
• festivals, rituals and practices
• Muslims in Britain today.

The suggestions below are designed to help teachers with different age groups to plan active RE work with a focus on Islam.

Teaching methods need to be varied and stimulating and make use of active learning strategies (see p.44–47).

Working with 6–8 year olds

- Listen to and re-tell stories about the life of Muhammad. Ask: What do you think is special about Muhammad for Muslims?

- Find out about how Muslims treat Al-Qur'an and why. Talk about what is so special for some people about words from Allah.

- Ask some questions about the daily prayers Muslims perform. Describe what happens and when. Talk about why prayer is important to Muslims.

- Talk about how Muslims celebrate family life and the birth of a baby. Ask: What is special about belonging?

- Watch a video about Hajj. Make links between the actions of hajjis/hajjas (pilgrims), stories from Al-Qur'an and the life of Muhammad. Talk about the ways in which Hajj reminds Muslims that all people are equal. Ask: How might the world today be different if everybody believed this? Why do people find it hard to treat people equally?

Working with 10–12 year olds

- Outline the story of the revelation of Al-Qur'an to Muhammad. Find out the difference between the authority of Al-Qur'an and the Hadith for Muslims. Ask a Muslim visitor some questions about how they use Al-Qur'an in their daily life. Ask: To whom do pupils turn for guidance? What books are special to them? In what ways are these books different from Al-Qur'an for Muslims?

- Talk about the Shahadah ('There is no god except Allah; Muhammad is the messenger of Allah') and use the 99 names of Allah to explore his attributes. Make links with belief in tawhid.

- Explore Islamic art, looking at shape, pattern, colour and calligraphy. Ask: What is their significance for Muslims, in the context of tawhid?

- Focus on the Muslim daily prayers (salat) as a time Muslims set aside for the worship of Allah. Ask: What do pupils consider sufficiently important to set aside time for? Consider what difference it might make to anyone's life to practise something five times a day and compare this with the effect of prayer on a Muslim's life.

- Explain how practising the five pillars might make a difference to individual Muslims and to the Muslim community (ummah).

- Investigate the design and purpose of a mosque and explain how and why the architecture and activities reflect Muslim beliefs.

- Discuss: Ibadah is a response to Allah in worship and in daily living. How does this affect Muslim values and choices?

- Evaluate diverse ideas from Muslim leaders about dealing with terrorism in the light of varied examples of the teaching on conflict found in Al-Qur'an and Hadith. Compare with Christian teachings and responses. Articulate arguments about how religions can bring peace and also cause conflict.

- Reflect: Iman is a Muslim's response in faith to Allah's revelation to Muhammad. What faith do pupils have, if any? What do they believe?

- Consider the concept of a society based on a religious code. Debate: What are the implications for individuals within an Islamic social and economic order?

- Research citizenship rights and the law within Islam. Evaluate the extent to which Muhammad can be considered a champion of equal rights. Reflect on the extent to which pupils themselves are 'champions of equal rights'.

- Justify two perspectives on British Muslim contributions to UK society in the light of the teaching of Al-Qur'an. Account for diversity of practice within British Islam, illustrating with examples.

A brief outline of Sikh belief and practice

Sikhism is the youngest of the major world religions. It is possible to describe the Sikh faith as a search for truth and truthful living. 'Truth is high, but higher still is truthful living', Guru Nanak said (Adi Granth 62).

The Gurus

Guru Nanak

Guru Nanak, the first of the Ten Sikh Gurus, lived in the Punjab region of India over 500 years ago. When he was about 30 years old, he received the call to preach the word of God, and travelled extensively to fulfil this mission. Sikhism is seen as an original, revealed religion. Many Sikhs prefer the term Sikhi to Sikhism, to show that this faith is not about a system of beliefs but a path to follow, a way of life. The term Sikh comes from the word sikhna, which means 'to learn'; hence a Sikh is a learner or disciple.

The Ten Gurus each contributed something to the developing faith and way of life that is the Sikh Dharam.

The Gurus

- Guru Nanak (1469–1539)
- Guru Angad (1504–52)
- Guru Amar Das (1479–1574)
- Guru Ram Das (1534–81)
- Guru Arjan (1563–1606)
- Guru Hargobind (1595–1644)
- Guru Har Rai (1630–61)
- Guru Har Krishan (1656–64)
- Guru Tegh Bahadur (1621–75)
- Guru Gobind Singh (1666–1708)

Guru Gobind Singh

Gobind Singh, the tenth Guru, founded the Sikh Khalsa at Baisakhi over 300 years ago (April 1699 CE). It was on this occasion that he encouraged his followers to 'take amrit' (nectar water) and become a Khalsa Sikh (or amritdhari), wearing what are now known as the five Ks as signs of this commitment. He also declared that the line of human gurus was to come to an end with him, and that the Sikh scriptures were to be the Sikhs' living Guru.

The Guru's teaching, now focused through the Guru Granth Sahib, emphasises belief in one God, the worship of God, universal love, peace and equality, and the importance of service (sewa).

Becoming a Khalsa Sikh

An amritdhari Sikh is one who has been initiated into the Khalsa. He or she will wear the five Ks, although not all who wear a turban and the five Ks are amritdhari (initiated). Many Sikhs are kesdhari (do not cut their hair or beard) without necessarily being amritdhari. There are also significant numbers of Sikhs who do not wear the five Ks. Note that the turban worn by many Sikhs is not one of the five Ks – this is worn to keep uncut hair tidy.

(When talking about becoming amritdhari, the terms baptise/baptism should be avoided since they have Christian connotations; instead initiate/initiation should be used.)

The five Ks are:

- kesh – uncut hair
- kara – a steel bracelet
- kanga – a wooden comb

- kaccha/kachera – cotton underwear
- kirpan – a steel sword.

Sikh beliefs, values and ethics

- There is one God, the supreme truth, creator and eternal (see the Mool/Mul Mantar, the opening verses of the Guru Granth Sahib, written by Guru Nanak and effectively a credal statement in Sikhism).
- Humans can find value in:

Naam Simran: meditation/recitation on the name of God

Kirat Karo: working hard and earning an honest day's living. Sikhs are encouraged to take part in charitable events

Vand Chakko: sharing one's food and earnings with the less fortunate.

The Guru Granth Sahib

The Sikh scriptures were first compiled by Guru Arjan, the fifth Guru. He ordered that all the texts be brought to him. He corrected some, rejected others that were not by the Gurus and did not contain the Sikh message, and added some songs and hymns. This task took over a year, and was completed in 1604 CE.

Guru Arjan's collection is called the Adi Granth, meaning 'first collection'.

Guru Gobind Singh revised the Adi Granth, adding the teaching of the Ten Gurus along with those of other holy men. In this book, the Guru Granth Sahib, he told his followers they would find all the guidance and inspiration they needed to live out their lives as Sikhs.

All Sikh ceremonies and services take place in the presence of the Guru Granth Sahib, which is treated with the greatest respect and honour.

The gurdwara

The gurdwara, the home of the Guru, is a place of worship housing the Guru Granth Sahib. This may be in someone's home, providing that he or she can care correctly for the Guru Granth Sahib. However, usually a gurdwara is a separate building that is not only for worship but as a focus for the life of the Sikh community.

In the gurdwara, the Sikh belief in equality is practised: anyone can participate in worship; no one is excluded; leading worship is open to all who can read the scriptures; all eat together in the langar (a free community kitchen).

Sikh ethics and practices

Ethical decisions are informed by:

- the principle of equality
- sewa; this 'selfless service' is the outworking of the worship of God, who is everywhere and in everyone.

The use of any sort of intoxicating drug (alcohol, tobacco and illicit drugs) is forbidden to Amrit Sikhs. Family life is very important – adultery is thoroughly condemned and divorce is frowned upon. Respect for and valuing life is important since life comes from God.

Sikhism developed in the Punjab, alongside Hindu and Muslim communities. Relationships with both communities were sometimes strained. One particular focus of Sikhism was challenging the discrimination and hierarchy of the caste system, hence the significance of all eating together at the langar, for example. The Sikh Gurus did not abolish the caste system, and many Sikhs still follow the Punjabi cultural idea of marrying within one's caste. There is a movement among a younger generation of Sikhs to challenge this as going against the egalitarian ideals of Sikhism, although this is not widespread.

Sikh practice includes:

- using stories from the Gurus' lives as examples of how to put faith into practice
- paying attention to the Gurus' teaching and reciting the Guru Granth Sahib
- celebrating festivals:
  - Gurpurbs, which are held in honour of one of the Ten Gurus, to celebrate their life or death (e.g. the birthdays of Guru Nanak and Guru Gobind Singh, and the martyrdoms of Guru Arjan and Guru Tegh Bahadur). Other anniversaries are also gurpurbs (e.g. the installation of the Adi Granth in 1604 CE).
  - Melas, which coincide with important Hindu festivals, but on which something important happened during the lives of one of the Gurus (e.g. Diwali, when Guru Hargobind was freed from captivity and insisted on taking with him all other captives).

The Sikh community

The Sikh community is reinforced by:

- the Sikh symbol, the Khanda
- the Khalsa, or brotherhood of Amrit Sikhs
- the wearing of the five Ks by some Sikhs
- worship in the gurdwara and sharing in the langar
- visiting the Golden Temple (Harmandir) at Amritsar.

Sikhism today

The first British gurdwara was opened in London in 1911 and there are now over 200 gurdwaras around the UK.

There are substantial Sikh populations in Greater London (especially Southall), Birmingham, Coventry, Leicester, Wolverhampton, Bradford, Cardiff and Glasgow.

Worldwide, there are more than 23 million Sikhs (mainly in the Punjab). In the UK, according to the 2011 census, there are 423,000 Sikhs (one of the largest Sikh communities outside the Punjab, along with Canada).

Sikhism in the classroom

The study of Sikhism is appropriate for pupils of any school age. It should be remembered that Sikhism is diverse and that there is a variety of practice in the UK and worldwide.

A balanced programme of study should include material about:

- the Gurus
- Sikh beliefs and values
- the gurdwara and community life
- festivals, rituals and practices
- Sikhs in Britain today.

The suggestions below are designed to help teachers with different age groups to plan active RE work with a focus on Sikhism. They are intended to be used flexibly and as part of active learning (see pp.44–47).

Working with 6–8 year olds

- Listen to stories about the Gurus' lives and about Sikh children in Britain today and respond with questions and ideas. Make a 'zigzag' book with appropriate text and illustrations about what is important to Sikhs.
- Look carefully at artefacts like the Khanda. Learn about their symbolism and significance.
- Think about the idea that all people are of equal value. Ask: Is this happening in the world today? How can we help make the world a more equal place?
- From six artefacts or pictures, select three that are used in a gurdwara. Make links with what is important for Sikhs.
- Give examples of angry and greedy behaviour, but also of gentleness and generosity. Ask: What behaviour would the Gurus approve or disapprove of? Why?

Working with 10–12 year olds

- Re-tell stories of the Gurus in various visual or written forms – focus on what Sikhs learn from such stories. Ask: What can I learn from them?
- Make collages on the theme of difference and equality. Think about the impact of Sikh teaching about equality on the way people in this country (or town, school, class) treat others. Ask: What would Guru Nanak say if he took our assembly?
- Outline Sikh beliefs expressed in the Mool/Mul Mantar. Talk about different Sikh names for God; explore ideas about God in other faiths and the pupils' own ideas. Conduct a survey about belief in God.
- Make booklets to illustrate a guided tour round a gurdwara, or a visit to Amritsar and the Harmandir (Golden Temple), describing ways in which the things Sikhs do show what they believe.
- Examine artefacts such as the five Ks and those associated with taking amrit, and write about the value of these to Sikhs. Talk about what it means to belong and what symbols of belonging pupils in the class have or use. Compare similarities and differences with Sikh symbols.
- Apply three sayings of Guru Nanak or one of the other Gurus found in the Guru Granth Sahib to pupils' own beliefs and lifestyle. Thoughtfully express pupils' responses to religious teachings.

Working with 14–16 year olds

- Consider the questions of Sikh identity in modern British culture, from religious and sociological perspectives. Investigate what it means to be a young Sikh in Britain today, including through meeting some young Sikhs.

- Examine the story of Guru Nanak's disappearance and revelation of the divine, and consider Sikh interpretations of it. Discuss the meaning of 'God' and religious experience and consider philosophical issues that arise.

- Use religious concepts from Sikhism to explain arguments for and against the reality of God, drawing balanced and well-substantiated conclusions.

- Analyse and compare the responses of Sikh, Christian and secular aid agencies to matters of injustice in the UK and beyond. Consider the motivations for action expressed; compare and conclude whether actions matter more than motivation.

- Devise various ethical and moral dilemmas. Explore how Sikhs might respond, putting the teaching of the Gurus into practice. Pupils are to give well-informed responses of their own in light of this learning.

A brief outline of non-religious worldviews

RE is not just for the religious, but for all pupils. Most pupils in schools in Britain today do not identify very closely, if at all, with a religious community, and so it is appropriate that RE should include consideration of some of the alternatives to religion which exist in our society. It is clear that it is not only religious people who take ethics seriously; there are various philosophies and approaches to life that have nothing to do with any particular religion, but call followers to lives of love and unselfishness.

These living belief systems can be grouped together as 'non-religious worldviews' or 'ethical life stances'. Their forms are often eclectic, but include everything from rationalist atheism and agnosticism, through post-Marxist accounts of humanity, to deliberately 'dis-traditioned' postmodern spiritualities or life stances.

People who feel at home with such descriptions do not all identify formally with Humanism, but the British Humanist Association is perhaps the most visible and organised non-religious ethical life stance to be seen in the nation's public life.

If the RE field of enquiry includes an exploration of the experience we share as humans, and an opportunity for a pupil to take a personal search further, it follows that teachers can plan to consider beliefs, values, celebrations and ideas from ethical traditions such as Humanism.

An ancient tradition

Humanism has a long history, and many great intellectuals from past centuries have influenced the modern Humanist tradition. These figures would include thinkers from classical civilisation such as Epicurus and Seneca, as well as enlightenment philosophers from Thomas Paine through John Stuart Mill to Bertrand Russell.

Notable contemporary Humanists in the UK include such public figures as Richard Dawkins, Stephen Fry, AC Grayling, Tim Minchin, Philip Pullman and Polly Toynbee.

A community dimension

Though relatively few Humanists belong to a Humanist organisation (the British Humanist Association has about 4000 members), the ideas of Humanism are very influential in the UK today, and many people recognise themselves when they hear Humanism described.

With an approach to life based on humanity and reason, Humanists recognise that moral choices are properly founded on human nature and experience alone. We value the truth, and consider facts as well as feelings in reaching a judgement. Humanists reject the idea of any supernatural agency intervening to help or hinder us.

British Humanist Association

Humanism briefly described
Humanists are people who:

- believe primarily in humanity
- hold that human nature is a remarkable product of the universe, but not the product of any divine creation, and that the human race can expect no help from any gods
- place their confidence in the power of human reason, goodwill and science to solve the problems that face us, and reject the power of prayer or worship
- accept the limitations of a lifetime and notice that we live on in the memories of others and in our achievements, but reject all ideas of rebirth, resurrection or eternal life
- when it comes to ethics, believe that their own reasoned sense of goodness and happiness should guide them to decide what is right for themselves and others
- are often concerned for the greatest happiness for the greatest number
- think it is best to make ethical decisions by looking at the individual case, not just by applying a hard-and-fast rule

- have often been active in working for human rights and get involved in a variety of social and ethical issues.

Those who identify themselves as Humanist may have special secular welcomes for a new baby, wedding ceremonies based on Humanist ideals and non-religious funerals. They may celebrate festivals in a secular way, whether this means joining in New Year celebrations with relish, or marking United Nations Day.

Humanism and ethics

Ethically, Humanism is often personal and individual, liberal, tolerant and rationally based. Humanists may be in favour of free choice in matters such as euthanasia or divorce, and may emphasise virtues such as truthfulness, generosity, democracy, tolerance, justice and co-operation. Humanists try to put the 'golden rule' into action: treat other people as you would like them to treat you.

Ten 'non-commandments'

In 1964 the Humanist Ronald Fletcher published a pamphlet called 'The Ten Non-Commandments: A Humanist Decalogue'. The text illustrates the spirit and feel of Humanism rather well, though, like other such texts, it requires a lot of unpacking and interpretation. It carries none of the authority of sacred texts in religious traditions, but most Humanists would be proud of that. It is suitable for the learning needs of pupils from about age 12.

The ten non-commandments are:

1. Never accept authority.
2. Base your conduct on simple, humane principles.
3. Strive to eliminate poverty.
4. Strive to eliminate war.
5. Do not be a snob.
6. In sexual behaviour, use your brains as well as your genitals, and always in that order.
7. Take the care necessary to enjoy family life and marriage.
8. Keep the law.
9. Commit yourself to active citizenship.
10. Have confidence in the modern world and your powers to improve it.

Five Humanist slogans

One local group of Humanists in Bromley has produced a set of posters to promote Humanist ideas. They have the following slogans on them:

1. Good without God
2. Morals without religion
3. Rites without religion
4. Ceremonies without superstition
5. Ethical atheism

 Non-religious traditions in the classroom

As RE explores human experience, beliefs and values, the non-religious approaches to life will be relevant at many points. This is reflected in the RE Council's Curriculum Framework for RE (2013), which talks about non-religious worldviews, giving Humanism as an example. It is also important to allow pupils with non-religious worldviews of their own, whether atheist or agnostic, to have the opportunity to reflect and think through their ideas in relation to other worldviews in RE.

Teachers can confidently include this material in the RE curriculum wherever it makes a contribution to the aims of RE as expressed in their statutory curriculum documentation e.g. locally agreed syllabus or diocesan guidelines.

A balanced study of Humanism should include:

• exploration of Humanist beliefs and values

• learning about some key historical and contemporary Humanist figures

• finding out about Humanist activities and ceremonies.

The suggestions below are designed to help teachers with different age groups to plan active RE work with a focus on non-religious worldviews such as Humanism. They are intended to be used flexibly and as part of active learning (see pp.44–47).

 Working with 6–8 year olds

• Look at the Humanist symbol of the Happy Human. Talk about what makes people happy and sad. Focus (perhaps through role play) on the ways people can help and support those who have sadness in their lives. Collage or artwork might be produced.

• Listen to, and talk about, stories that exemplify human goodness without reference to any god.

• Collect a list of some things that are precious but that money can't buy. Use the list to think and talk about values and what matters most to us.

• 'Do to others as you would like them to do to you.' Draw cartoons to illustrate the 'golden rule'. Talk about how people feel when they are treated fairly and unfairly.

• Compare a 'secular' celebration like New Year or a birthday with a religious one. Ask: What is the same, and what is different?

Working with 10–12 year olds

- Learn to use the terms 'agnostic', 'atheist', 'secular' and 'non-religious' in speaking about issues of meaning, purpose and ethics in any RE context.
- 'Do to others as you would like them to do to you.' Compare versions of this rule found in many different contexts. Apply it to some moral problems. Illustrate how 'morality without God' can use this idea.
- Examine the ways Humanists celebrate key steps through life and explore similarities and differences compared with religious ceremonies.
- Use the five Humanist slogans on page 110 to get pupils to think about meanings, symbols and visual expression. Ask them to devise posters which illustrate the slogans, using non-religious symbolism and natural images.
- Explain how Christians and Humanists share (e.g.) three similar ideas about ethics but have opposite ideas about God and life after death. Discuss, argue or debate the reasons Humanists use to support their rejection of religious ideas like God, prayer, revelation or life after death.

Working with 14–16 year olds

- Research the ways key figures in Humanism have put their ideas into action. Examples could include Thomas Paine, Simone de Beauvoir or Bertrand Russell.
- Study the 'Humanist Decalogue' (Fletcher) given on page 110. Compare it to some other codes for living from within religions but also other 'alternative' versions from Humanists. Ask: what if everyone lived like this? What kinds of families, schools, communities would we get?
- Analyse Humanist ethical ideas and reasoning about issues such as sexuality, euthanasia or world poverty and ask pupils to articulate their own positions on these issues.
- Evaluate three criticisms of religion made by Humanists and three criticisms of Humanism made by religious people.
- Apply Ninian Smart's seven dimensions of religion to Humanism and analyse the question: 'Is Humanism a religion?' Ask: Does Humanism have social, ethical, doctrinal, material, ritual, mythological and experiential dimensions? What are they?
- Discuss, analyse and respond to the place of Humanism in relation to world religions in an essay. A possible title: 'Humanism in Britain is not really an alternative to religion. It's more like an anti-religious pressure group.' How far do you agree?

Resourcing RE: how do we decide what to use in RE?

What makes a good resource?

A study conducted by Warwick University into the sorts of books used in RE found that most RE teachers used books as a factual basis but went far wider in resourcing their lessons.[41] It was found that although most textbooks do not have a strong community cohesion or personal values agenda, most RE teachers wish their lessons to meet these wider aims as well as transmit solid knowledge about religious beliefs and traditions. Teachers supplement their lessons with information from the internet, magazines, artefacts, visiting speakers and, of course, the pupils' own experiences of religious life. This was the case in 2009 and is even more so now, when teachers routinely use the internet in their classrooms, whether to access YouTube or news reports, play clips from TV shows and films or play popular songs, or to access online content designed specifically for schools. But an easy-to-access resource may not be a good one, so we will consider here what *does* make a good resource.

Books

Books are still the staple of most teachers' classroom diet, but there is an enormous range to choose from. A book should be interesting, engaging and of genuine use to the teacher. Below are five elements to look for when choosing books – whether individual copies as resources in primary schools, or perhaps as textbooks in secondary schools.

- **Integrity:** does the book have integrity in its representation of the religion in question? For example, does a book on Hinduism have a Hindu author or advisers, or depict a real British Hindu family? The Warwick investigation into RE text books reported that 'Academic reviewers and faith consultants pointed out a high number of errors and points for criticism in the coverage of religions.'[42] Carry out an internet search on a book's author and consultant advisers to find out the extent of their expertise and authority. Do images reflect diversity of belief accurately, or do they reinforce stereotypes?

- **Engagement and challenge:** where appropriate, are the questions and subject matter of the book both engaging and challenging for the age group? Factual information should lead to questions that require a deeper level of thought than recall and should invite engagement with issues and perspectives. Are the images, photographs and diagrams eye-catching, interesting and relevant? Are aids to understanding provided?

- **Educational standpoint:** what is the educational standpoint of the resource? For example, it may not be appropriate to use books written for a church audience to teach Christianity in a non-religious setting such as the classroom, since these resources assume a believing audience. However, it is possible to explore such resources as examples of material from within a tradition.

- **Depth:** the Warwick report found that world religions other than Christianity can often be presented in a rather superficial manner. The focus is often on external characteristics of religious people, clothes and buildings, rather than deeper theology or spirituality. Make sure you choose books that have depth as well as colour.

- **Value for money:** do the books support pupil learning? Are the books a valuable addition to the school library due to their scope, presentation and educational quality?

---

[41] *Materials Used to Teach About World Religions in Schools in England*, DCSF Summary Report RB197 (University of Warwick 2010).

[42] Ibid., p.2.

Video, film and TV

Whether YouTube, clips from films and TV shows or films made for the purposes of education, teachers use an incredibly wide range of video in the classroom, for a range of purposes. In a subject like RE, which is about the people of the world, video can be of enormous value in bringing faraway places, languages, traditions and rituals to life with unparalleled immediacy. The BBC Bitesize website has a wide range of clips for RE (www.bbc.co.uk/education). Channel 4's clipbank (for secondary) (clipbank.channel4learning.com), TrueTube (www.truetube.co.uk) and REQuest (request.org.uk) are also sources of appropriate clips. Keep an eye out for documentary seasons connected to RE topics. For example, in 2013, Channel 4 aired a set of three documentaries called *A Very British Ramadan*, showing the lives of British Muslims as they prepared to fast. All of these resources offer incredibly valuable access to people and places to support learning. Some tips:

- **Documentary clips:** when using factual clips about a person, group of people, religious event or location, make sure they are woven into the fabric of your lesson. Make sure your pupils know enough before they watch the clip to get the most from it. Use the clip to deepen understanding of a topic by setting it *within* a set of learning activities. Don't be afraid to return to the clip another time to recap, consolidate key information, test them, or find out if their ideas have changed since you first watched it. Don't just sit back once you have pressed 'play': make video clips work hard for you!

- **Feature film clips:** in a subject like RE, which is about big human values and big human emotions, using a dramatic, exciting or emotional scene from a feature film is always tempting. However, the clip used must *support* the concepts under investigation, not *detract* from them by being similar but not really the same. Before you use a feature film or TV clip, ask yourself if it really says the same thing as the religious teaching or key idea you are exploring. The same warning goes for using pop songs in your lessons. While songs can be used incredibly effectively, they must support the learning and provide a way to go deeper into key religious ideas. However, when you find the right clip and weave it into a challenging lesson, the results can be spectacular.

Images

Online news and image search engines provide a constant source of fresh, new images to use in your lessons. So much in RE can be unlocked through the visual, through ancient art and sculpture, famous paintings of religious themes, architecture and art in places of worship, modern art forms and images of religious people and events. Keep your images fresh and up to date. You might need to tweak your lesson plan when you update an image, but it gives pupils the message that religion is of immediate contemporary relevance. Create your own images using digital cameras (or smart phones!) and use them in pupils' work or displays. Do not use an image solely for decoration but, as with videos, as a resource in its own right that must work hard in your lesson.

Responding to images

Pupils could be asked to respond to an image in a variety of ways:

- Thoughtful questions, e.g. What do you notice? What will happen next? What does the artist want to say? What questions would you ask the artist? What religious theme does this image express or comment on? What does the image teach you?

- Ask pupils to go beyond the image and describe what they think might be going on around the image, beyond the part that they can see.

- Get pupils to trade places with the people in the image, setting up a 'freeze-frame' depicting the scene. The rest of the class ask questions about information, meaning, interpretations and feelings associated with the image.

- Hide part of the image and get pupils to speculate about what is missing, using evidence in the image and their own interpretative skills.
- Compare similarities and differences between varied images of the same subject. Which one captures the essence of the story/idea/concept and how?

Artefacts

Artefacts engender a desire to know what they represent. Pupils of all ages love to handle artefacts, although you will have to set ground rules, as they may be sacred objects to members of the faith. Use artefacts as a 'way in' to a religious theme, or compare artefacts from different faiths to make points about similarities and differences; for example, compare Islamic prayer beads and Catholic rosary beads. Artefacts can be an effective entry point to religious texts, making textual analysis meaningful. For example, learning about the prayer scroll inside tefillin and mezuzot in Jewish practice will lead pupils quite naturally to reading passages from Torah. As with all resources, make artefacts work for you. Weave their exploration into a lesson to aid a deeper understanding of a religious theme.

Websites

There are many websites that provide excellent sources of information from within and outside diverse traditions. As always, discernment needs to be used to assess the suitability of websites for the age group of your class, and whether they are safe for use in school. Here are some questions you might need to ask so that you can judge whether and how to use a site.

- From where does the site originate?
- Can you identify the organisation that supports the site?
- Is this a religious/non-religious organisation?
- Does this have an impact on the content?
- Is the site biased? How do you know?
- Does it support a particular religious, spiritual or ethical position?
- Is it clear who produced the material (e.g. in an 'About Us' section)?
- Can you contact them should you want to?
- What is the academic credibility of the site?
- Does it attribute sources?
- Does it cite evidence?
- Does it include a bibliography/webography?
- When was the site last updated? Does this matter?
- Is the site, including any advertising that appears on it, acceptable in terms of gender, creed, race, sexuality, age and values?

Further help

There is substantial guidance on resources, including checklists for assessing the value and purpose of a whole range of resources, on the NATRE website:

www.natre.org.uk/about-re/guidance-on-resources/introduction

RE Today publishes a wide range of classroom resources for all age groups. Full details available here: shop.retoday.org.uk

The Warwick/DCSF report into materials used in schools is available here: www2.warwick.ac.uk/fac/soc/ces/research/wreru/research/completed/dcsf

Index

Index

REtoday the magazine for the Religious Education community

REtoday magazine is published by RE Today Services, which works nationally and internationally to support Religious Education in schools. It is committed to the teaching of the major world faiths in Religious Education, and to an accurate and fair representation of their beliefs, values and practices in all its teaching materials.

The breadth of work includes:

★ offering professional development and consultancy services through our team of RE Advisers
★ leading regional, national and international courses for teachers, pupils and others interested in education
★ research and curriculum development
★ supporting the National Association of Teachers of Religious Education (NATRE)
★ writing and producing RE resources, including *REtoday* magazine.

Published termly, **REtoday** magazine connects you to a breadth of ideas and diverse thinking to benefit you in the classroom.

To find out more go to www.retoday.org.uk

Inside you will find:

Opinion – RE professionals, theologians and people of faith inform and expand on current thinking

For the classroom – tried-and-tested RE lesson ideas for EYFS and 5–19s

Instant RE – quick, easy and effective ideas to use immediately

Professional REflection – a rich assembly of articles, reviews and commonplace thoughts to interest and stimulate reflection

For the staffroom – up-to-date discussion pieces helping to equip and engage you and your colleagues

Events and resources – news, courses, conferences and reviews of books and resources

Additional online resources – available through the dedicated download code.

This creative resource is packed with current themes and articles which will inform, challenge and inspire you to teach better RE!

REtoday
The magazine for the Religious Education community

In this issue

Peter Tatchell
on equal love

Al Murray:
The Pub Landlord on the Golden Rule

What's the problem?
Sin, suffering and the problems of RE analysed (and solved?)

Professional REflection:
Bill Gent introduces ...
a selection of articles, reviews and perspectives to interest and challenge

also...

25+
classroom ideas
ready to try for primary and secondary RE

6
different views
on what's wrong with humanity

Incorporating
Professional REflection
formerly
REsource

Sara Pascoe:
'RE is a fantastic tool'

For the classroom

...Christian community, which ...experienced in the same way ...ere else. The malades had amazing ...to tell.

...ynne Wallis is Head of RE, ...chael's Grammar School, ...n Finchley.

...ffney, 17: Lourdes is a ...different world to the one that ...ndon and that's part of the ...I love it so much. In Lourdes ...equal and even though ...ny people who have faced ...ip, there is a great sense of ...e chance to help people ...n their faith and optimism ...am really grateful for; it ...n sense of faith and gives ...gement to live my faith ...l Cap in Lourdes makes ...re part of something ...n your own world and ...od feeling.

...17: By helping and ...ly on a physical and ...e to realise the value ...r listening to Cardinal ...e recent euthanasia ...stand the reasons ...sanctity of all life. ...nstrated the power ...be and sustenance ...e of the people I ...me to gain a clearer ...life. Returning to ...ne, with maturity ...ny experience ...ore focused on ...living life to

...e days leading ...rvous- not ...t also knowing ...erving as ...d be high. ...les, I had ...experience. I ...with my

For the classroom:

❶ Read the five student commentaries above. List all the activities, and all the emotions they speak about.

❷ 'Red Caps wanted. No pay, long hours, hard work.' Why did they go, and what did they get out of it? Write an advert for next year's pilgrimage.

❸ Some people believe in spiritual healing, and see Lourdes as a place where this is more likely to happen.

MORE THAN... 101 GREAT IDEAS

The perfect accompaniment to *Religious Education: The Teacher's Guide*

More Than ... 101 Great Ideas provides a rich collection of tried-and-tested practical classroom strategies to support spiritual and moral development in the RE classroom for 5–16s.

These strategies expand on ideas outlined in the chapter 'Active learning in RE: what are the benefits?' and the practical suggestions on pages 45–47 of *Religious Education: The Teacher's Guide*.

Act – strategies to provide pupils with opportunities to express their ideas, understanding and questions in RE in an active and expressive way, through drama, body sculpture, mime and much more

Create – ideas to energise pupils' thinking in a creative way, for example through art, collage, music, drawing, ICT, storytelling, poetry and photography

Enquire – a wide variety of strategies that enable pupils to develop their ideas, understanding and ability to ask good questions in RE through enquiry and solving problems

Reflect – strategies to help pupils engage with religious and spiritual materials for themselves and respond with their own increasing insights through discussion, visual learning, values clarification, and other methods

Talk – teachers who want their lessons to be places of spiritual and moral development need good strategies to get pupils talking purposefully; strategies include debate, careful observation, and dialogue using religious language accurately

Think – a range of strategies to develop pupils' ideas, understanding and questions in a reflective and thoughtful way: clarifying ideas, valuing the opinions of others, and deep thinking about concepts and issues

Write – imaginative and structured strategies to help pupils develop through the study of the writings of others and written responses of their own, evaluative essay writing, and distinguishing between a variety of beliefs and interpretations.

Within each strategy are a helpful quick 'useful for' guide and 'see also' references, linking to other strategies in the publication

Pupil activity sheets accompany these strategies and are downloadable from the RE Today website when you purchase *More Than . . . 101 Great Ideas*.

This is an excellent book and online resource, overflowing with ideas to help you in the RE classroom and also inspire primary and secondary teachers across the breadth of the subjects they teach.

Buy your copy at shop.retoday.org.uk

RE Today
Services

Visit: www.retoday.org.uk • Email: sales@retoday.org.uk